THIS IS MY BODY

A Story of Sickness and Health

Jennie Hogan

CANTERBURY
PRESS

Norwich

© Jennie Hogan 2017

First published in 2017 by the Canterbury Press Norwich
Editorial office
3rd Floor, Invicta House
108–114 Golden Lane
London EC1Y 0TG, UK

Canterbury Press is an imprint of Hymns Ancient & Modern Ltd
(a registered charity)

H
Y
M
N
S
Ancient
& Modern EST 1861

Hymns Ancient & Modern® is a registered trademark of
Hymns Ancient & Modern Ltd
13A Hellesdon Park Road, Norwich,
Norfolk NR6 5DR, UK

www.canterburypress.co.uk

Scripture quotations are from the New Revised Standard Version of
the Bible, Anglicized Edition, copyright © 1989, 1995 by the Division
of Christian Education of the National Council of the Churches of
Christ in the USA. Used by permission. All rights reserved.

Prayers for Compline are taken from *Common Worship:
Services and Prayers* for the Church of England. Published by Church
House Publishing, 2000 © The Archbishops' Council 2000
copyright@churchofengland.org.uk

British Library Cataloguing in Publication data

A catalogue record for this book is available
from the British Library

978 1 84825 948 5

Typeset by Manila Typesetting Company
Printed and bound in Great Britain by
CPI Group (UK) Ltd

*This book is dedicated to my parents,
John and Pamela Hogan*

Contents

Acknowledgements

This book was originally conceived as a joint project between me and my friend, Sarah Eynstone. Sarah and I trained for the priesthood together at Westcott House, Cambridge. She was a very driven, original and prophetic priest. Whenever we met we would talk about our health and our faith, as well as our work in the Church as clergy.

Very sadly, Sarah died in 2016. In telling my story here, Sarah has been a significant influence. I learnt such a lot from her and I will always cherish the many conversations we shared.

My love and thanks go to Amy for her patience, insight and gentleness.

Thanks also to my parents for their tireless support.

Foreword

That human life is precarious is a commonplace, but to some is given a deeper understanding than others. And it's an often repeated reflection that in a wordy society, living our lives online, we have become too detached from our bodies: their frailties, the ways in which they change over time, the reality of ageing, and the inevitability of death.

This detachment is magnified in some strands of Christian theology, which prefers to suppress bodily preoccupations in the service of a higher spiritual calling. This book, part autobiography, part theological reflection, refuses to collude with this separation.

This book bears witness to both the beauty and brutality of living; it's a message from the front line of the borderland between sickness and health. Jennie Hogan writes unsparingly about her body, which she has had to get to know in ways she can never have wanted but has somehow gratefully received. And she writes passionately about the Christian tradition in which she finds both solace and challenge. While hers is a story unflinchingly told of physical suffering from a very young age, she refuses to let this suffering become detached from equally powerful spiritual realities. In this way, her reflections are truly holistic in a way that many attempts to address "mind, body, spirit" simply don't achieve.

She resists neat arcs, swerves away from any hint of self-pity, and instead gives us a raw account of a life that has learned to trust God because nothing physical can be trusted. It's a moving account of her own story in her own words, re-interpreting the sequence she says she has inherited – of "disaster, bravery, combat and triumph".

Alongside the bracing descriptions of medical invasions are the most delightful and witty vignettes of primary school, theological college and the curious privilege of ministry in the Church of England. It is a book of tears and a book of trust. A book about the enduring love of family and the undefeated love of women.

Jennie tells a story of a body and a spirit that seem to be both vulnerable and resilient, a story that encompasses the violence of breaking bones and the peace of silent godly contemplation. And, in the end, it's a story shot through with unvanquished hope. We who are afraid to die, should salute her.

Lucy Winkett

Preface

This is my body is uttered in cries the moment a baby leaves the womb; *this is my body* naked flesh announces inside operating theatres; *this is my body* is spoken and unspoken when two people fall in love; *this is my body* are the words of Jesus mouthed by robed men and women standing at altars; *this is my body* say bent knees and hands pressed together in prayer.

This Is My Body is a story of pain, trauma, illness, recovery and transformation. Hopefully this story will mirror other tales of sickness, suffering and the search for making sense of it all.

My body, our bodies and the body of Christ are the beginning and end of this book. It is written for those with or without belief. We all have bodies and each one of them tells its own story. It is my intention that readers will see and feel and live with their bodies differently.

I

Weakness

I was baptized at St Aidan's Church in Mill Hill, near Blackburn, Lancashire. My maternal grandfather, Harold Holt, was the vicar. The christening took place on a Sunday afternoon with water that came from the River Jordan. I was always amazed by this when I was growing up: I was baptized with water from the same river that Jesus was dipped in. There is a square sunny photograph of me, less than six months old, held in my father's arms beside the church door, surrounded by my family.

Besides breaking the taboo of Roman Catholicism in my parents' mixed marriage, and the vicar sharing a quarter of my genes, my baptism was very ordinary. Not many years later, benign Church of England churchgoing, coupled with the typical religious apathy of the baby boomer generation, created – for me at least – a God who was male, nice, absent and, well . . . easily forgettable.

There was probably tea, chatter and vicar's-wife-homemade-cake in the vicarage following the splash of water at the font and anointing on my forehead with the holy oil of Chrism. My grandfather would have looked into my eyes and said: 'Christ claims you as his own. Receive the sign of the cross.' I looked completely healthy, completely normal. My sister, Rebecca, was already walking and beginning to talk, so two children made the family almost complete (no male progeny), therefore the cosy private service on that Sunday afternoon seemed like a comforting celebration of family life.

Everyone at my Church of England primary school was baptized. It was as regular and routine as vaccinations: not entirely comfortable but good for you. The unquestioned ubiquity of baptism until relatively recently may have watered down the stark and bold claims made in the baptismal rite. And yet, while a baptism *is* an opportunity to celebrate the birth of a child, if we watch and listen to what is going on it is a moment when a powerless child is symbolically buried with Christ in order to share in his resurrection. In baptism, taking on the likeness of Jesus, which begins in that ritual, is a call for those still getting to know the baby to look at the child's face, and face for themselves the reality that the ball of perfection at the centre of everyone's attention will never be completely perfect at all.

The downy head touched so tenderly by my grandfather would ten years later have a scar snaked around half of it. The thick red hair that would grow would be shaved off in haste, a blade would slit open the scalp, a hammer would crack open the skull and clips would cut off bleeding brain cells in the hope of saving my life – regardless of what state I would wake up in: blind, paralysed or permanently vegetative. Just not claimed by death. Not yet.

When the child gurgles during the christening ceremony she is an embodiment of a pure gift. Of course, no one wishes for suffering, but the water of baptism symbolizes chaos and death as well as life. Everyone seems to expect perfection. We spend our lives aching and striving for it. But only Christ is perfect. However, our unique human identity is offered as a gift through Christ, who himself is offered as a gift to the world. If we turn away from our self-obsession and observe the face and fate of Jesus we can see our human dependence, vulnerability and death mirrored there. It is easy and understandably preferable to focus on loveliness and ignore the terrifying reality of suffering that every one of us must experience in one way or another. There are so many ways to suffer, so many kinds of pain and so many ways to die. Christianity starts out cute and comforting: the baby Jesus born in the silent night. But if we carry on listening to the story of Jesus it very soon gets quite uncomfortable, ugly, gory and terrifying. But that is not how the story of Jesus ends and it is not, if we dare to believe it, how our story ends either.

One of my school teachers got married at half term, during my final year at primary school. I was in the church choir and we sang at her wedding. Two days later I decided to go to bed early, which was unusual. Once in bed I couldn't sleep, *I could not sleep*. My head hurt. I felt very sick and my cheeks were burning.

Giving in, I went to my parents' bedroom, going round to my mother's side. It wasn't the first time; occasionally when I was a much younger child I would go into their bedroom if I couldn't sleep and would lie sandwiched between them. But still, with my age now in double figures, it must have been quite a shock to see me there with blazing red cheeks and fear in my eyes.

'I don't feel well.'

I was confused, but I don't remember being afraid; being ill was not so unusual. Gentle and unquestioning, my mum welcomed me into the middle of their bed, right in the middle. But as soon as I lay down I vomited and turned hot, very hot, and began to squirm. I don't remember the pain so much; but the terror, the *dreadful* knowledge that engulfed me as night, safe night, half-term holiday night, was settling down; I knew it too young.

'I'm going to die,' I told my dad.

My mother was downstairs on the telephone. I could hear her speaking in the same way she spoke as a school teacher at the end of her tether. She had assumed her professional manner, half-dressed and in the dark, to get quick results and perhaps to mask her own worry.

'Someone please come and see our daughter. She isn't right. She's really not well at all. Please, can someone be sent to help us?'

My mother hadn't heard my prophecy. Was it a question or an announcement? My dad understood that *that word* had to be eliminated from that room before she returned. He was sitting up in bed with his back to the wall beside me and stroking my head which felt like a cannon ball ready to explode.

'Don't be so silly, Jennie. You're not going to die!'

But I don't think I believed him. I sensed for the first time that my father was scared. He couldn't hide behind the veneer of omniscience most parents develop because he could sense the prospect of death too.

I had not thought much about death before then. The benign services in church had offered me worship songs of joy, not versed me in hope in the resurrection of the dead. I had not been told about purgatory or hell, but I knew that life was better than death. Struggling to breathe in my parents' bed I sensed death that was coming to get me and I would have to fight it. Building up inside me was a black, dark, screeching, thunderous force that I had to beat. I was used to winning: I was the captain of the netball team and we won the league that year; I liked to challenge the boys who dared to boast that they could ride their bikes faster than me. I was – in my mind at least – the best roller skater in Lancashire. But this monstrous force was something else; should I just let it devour me and finish me off, so soon, so young? This threat was a rampaging enemy, something to be very, very afraid of. *Come on then*, I thought, *I will take you on.*

It was the GP on call who came, not an ambulance. I have a faint memory of him coming into the bedroom. He was slightly overweight and wearing a grey jacket.

'Just give her sugar and salt solution,' he instructed.

He probably thought my parents were uneducated time wasters. My parents, grateful recipients of a doctor's precious time, especially at night, did as he said. But the simple low-tech solution did not work. The moment he left the fluid spewed out on to the bed. I got worse. I was hunched on my hands and knees, rocking and swaying to make way for vomit, snot, saliva; sweat poured from my body. I had no control over what my body was doing; it did not seem to be mine any more.

The doctor returned. The word meningitis was uttered. What else could it be? Why was a fit girl suddenly writhing like an injured shot animal in bed and gripping her scalp with both hands? This girl who, only the day before, had climbed up a mountain in the Lake District.

I do not remember an ambulance coming because by the time it arrived the pain had blinded me. They took me to the local hospital and doctors confirmed that I did not have meningitis. It took a while for someone to suggest having a look at my brain; I would need a scan, they said. They looked and saw immediately that there was something abnormal. They must have panicked; no one there wanted to touch the insides of an 11-year-old's head. I was becoming less mobile, more absent. An ambulance rushed me and my parents 70 miles south to somewhere more specialized, the Royal Children's Hospital in Pendlebury, Manchester. Mr R. A. C. Jones, a brain surgeon, took charge. I was scanned again, monitored and stabilized with drugs. My brain was haemorrhaging blood.

Buoyant, healthy cells, making me *me*, were dying, drowning, disappearing for ever. It was a malformation of the brain; there was a malformed connection between the arteries and the veins on the right temporal lobe. A tangled nest of blood vessels, probably formed in the womb, had ruptured, dilated and disrupted the regular flow of blood, causing intracranial bleeding. A quarter of people die when the brain bleeds like this. Permanent catastrophic brain damage, sight loss, paralysis and much more harm often occur, particularly when the bleeding isn't stopped quickly.

As I was examined my mum paced the corridor, unable to sit still. She saw the surgeon in waiting sitting at a table, half hiding – with his face to the wall. He was reading the *Telegraph* and snapping open a Kit Kat. She resisted the instinct to run towards him, grab his shoulders and shake him, insisting he should rush to the operating theatre immediately. Although she could not save my life perhaps he could, better than anyone else in the north-west of England that early dawn. My dad kept pace with the trolley I was lying on as I was wheeled to a bright spotless sanctuary. Lying supine, stilled by sedatives, I could make out cartoon images and characters on the ceiling. It was not at all like the Sistine Chapel I would marvel at in my twenties. Donald Duck, Tigger, Mickey Mouse grinned down to make me . . . happy? At home? And there between me and the zany ceiling was my father staring down putting on a valiant smile, but his chin trembled as he joked that it seemed silly for him to be wearing the same outfit as the doctors. His work uniform was a regulation bottle-green smock he wore to deliver pies to chip shops. I went away to a deep sleep and returned to consciousness four hours later, an embodiment of misfortune, miracle, misery and mystery.

In the operating theatre the neurosurgeon cracked open part of my skull, extracted a portion of it, resected and clipped the damaged mess of blood vessels. Mr Jones sewed me up and told my dumbstruck parents that they would just have to wait and see.

Doctors are eloquent at the unsaid. Their preferred lexicon is the euphemism: *'There may be some deficits.'* She may be in a vegetative state; she may not be able to speak, walk, see or think.

'I do have some concerns.' She may well die.

'Everything should go to plan.' There are so many things that could go wrong.

'We'll do everything we can.' I'm terrified.

My parents weren't given any numbers to add up. Later they learned the statistics of just how many people with intracranial bleeding, caused by the kind of malformation I had, die.

Pamela and John Hogan, aged 36 and 34 respectively, kept a vigil. Holding hands, stunned and made speechless by sorrow, they circled the hospital in the Salford rain.

'Who is the prime minister?' enquired a doctor, staring down at me beside my bed.

'Margaret Thatcher.' I knew the answer but it is a bizarre question to ask a groggy girl who turned 11 only a month earlier.

Then he asked, 'Where are you, Jennie?'

'On the golf course.' He and the nurses surrounding me laughed nervously, but at least I knew what a question was, and I could talk, and think. And I had been on a golf course earlier that week developing a swing of my own. So some cells fired, certain connections were being made. There was an air of hope.

The Garden of Eden

The LORD God took the man and put him in the garden of Eden to till it and keep it.

Genesis 2.15

Eden is a land of sheer liberty and beauty: there is no pain, sorrow or fear. Adam and Eve are God's utter delight: they are the crown of all creation. They inhabit a lush land made perfect by its beneficent creator. Existence is to be enjoyed, not endured. Adam and Eve are encouraged to revel and play together.

✠

Childhood is never perfect; we all bear scars, some more than others. Most of us spend our early years playing; that's how we learn to be human and discover who we are. Unlike every other creature we are utterly dependent on others and require endless attention. Touch, sound, smell, food – we cannot get enough comfort when we are very young. Babies' desperate fragility can be terrifying for some people, including me, perhaps because it reminds us of our own fragility and our own childhood. I don't have children but when I hear certain cries from babies – the weary wailing sort of cries – I begin to panic because they are familiar sounds. I have made them myself many times, not only as a baby, but as a child, a teenager and a grown-up. I still make wailing sounds now sometimes when I am ill. My body seems to make them *for me*. They arise from somewhere within, beyond my control.

Very young children's bodies are beautiful in their fresh and lively physical perfection; but this perfection is delicately poised beside the possibility of pain and loss. So many things may go wrong, and how would we find what the problem is when a baby can be held in only two stretched-out hands? There is a desire for life expressed as hunger for food and people. The miniature glory of a baby, fed and loved, should be seen as Adam and Eve saw Eden: a delight and the essence of the glorious bounty from God.

In an ideal world we could all think of our early years as a garden of Eden. We're watched, nurtured, tended, protected and carefully guided towards growth. Even if it isn't perfect – and of course it never really can be – childhood is hopefully a time of innocence. We soon learn to need, to be loved, to name things and learn to know ourselves through play. Loving attention encourages us to grow and move further along our unique journey. Although we don't like to imagine it, the journey will not always be pleasant.

A baby's skin is thin, perfectly smooth, sometimes translucent. Bones feel fragile, malleable even, and lolling heads call out our instinct to care and protect. We push away the thought that things can go wrong, but these fleshy bundles of perfection can't be owned, and can't be held in a mother's arms for ever. At some point a child's nakedness is covered and she has to be led out of the garden of innocence.

A pervasive fear of the body's delicacy and vulnerability never fades. Curiosity, pride, arrogance and foolishness put an end to innocence and freedom in the story of the garden of Eden in the book of Genesis – the first book in the Bible – where the story of God in relation to humanity begins. The story of God's creation and the world and the tale of Adam and Eve is a myth which was created, written, retold, and remains with us now because it is *true*. This is how we are.

✠

My parents stayed with me in the high dependency ward. They slept on chairs, drinking bad coffee and living on sandwiches and crisps. Eyes still closed, no full sentences yet, I could smell the vinegar and hear the crunch. Although I did not recognize it at that moment I had lost some peripheral vision on my left visual field so my sense of smell was animal-sharp.

Rebecca, my only sibling, was sent to stay with our grandparents, but they visited every evening. She is only 18 months older than me; I don't remember her speaking very much to me in the hospital. She was probably terrified, wondering whether she had inherited a malformed brain too. My grandfather had retired as a vicar that year. In his work as a parish priest he was used to sitting at bedsides, waiting quietly, hoping, praying, trying to stay awake in stuffy hospital wards. Other people visited me and my parents: neighbours, family friends, and they brought balloons, chocolate, nightdresses with bears stitched on the front to complement the hospital's efforts at paediatric cheerfulness. Mr Heaps, the head teacher of my primary school, visited. Some people couldn't stomach the mess, the dried blood, the fluid sacs, the bleeps and wires. I was an attraction and had become a symbol of relief: 'Isn't technology wonderful?' people said and smiled, rendered wide-eyed by science.

The nurses – all female at that time – switched between professional and maternal roles with practised ease. A fixed stare at the upside-down watch testing a pulse, then the gentle stroking of a hand on my hair, the part of it that remained. I had bandages on my head covering the stitches at the back. I had not asked to see myself in a mirror, but no one had offered either and I should have been suspicious because when I eventually looked at myself in the mirror I was shocked by what I saw.

Before I could go home I needed to have a test called an angiogram. This meant sedation and further treatment in the operating theatre with the cartoon pictures on the ceiling. It was not explained to me what would happen but I sensed that it would not be comfortable. I soon realized that the more tenderly the doctors spoke beforehand, the more traumatic the procedure would be. The night before the procedure I wore a brand-new nightdress, a gift from a neighbour. I wet the bed. I was a baby again and that silly bear embroidered on the front of the nightgown emphasized it. Never much of a crier, nor a daddy's girl, I cried, huddled on my father's knee in the morning before they wheeled me away. I didn't want to have things done to me in the theatre again, and I didn't want to be put to sleep and never wake up.

I was too grown-up to be properly cradled, too young to be told the explicit details of this procedure where iodine dye is navigated by a catheter through the groin towards the brain so that blood flow can be scanned in high definition.

'It looks pretty safe to me!' Mr R. A. C. Jones trumpeted when he visited me in the ward afterwards.

I was sent home after two weeks. My scar begged to be stared at. Two angry red lines, curved from the back of my head towards my right ear, were fixed together by clips and stitches. I was taken to choose a wig from a shop on King Street, the most glamorous street in Manchester. I picked one that looked like a rough copper helmet, a lot like the hair I had before. I looked ridiculous, but nobody said so. I couldn't see the scar because it was at the back of my head and I didn't ask to get a better look. I felt triumphant, a winning soldier, so I felt no shame. My scars and my shaved red hair were battle scars. What a brave girl, they kept saying, and each affirmation felt like being given a medal.

I was sent back to school. It was not explained that I might become different, or experience pain; no one hinted that I might have residual effects such as memory loss, problems with words, numbers, hearing, touch and chronic fatigue. No one told me, or my parents, that there was a one in four chance that I might have another bleed. Once or twice strange twinkling lights flickered before my eyes and briefly darkened my vision. I mentioned it to my parents and we agreed that it must just be my brain knitting together.

I regained my captainship of the netball team; I played Nancy in the school production of the musical *Oliver*, drawing gasps of admiration not least because this Nancy did not have long hair and my scar was lit up by the spotlights as I crooned solos and danced with Bill Sykes.

'Well, Jennie,' pronounced Mr R. A. C. Jones, at an outpatients check-up a year later, 'you're clearly doing *so* well. I don't think we need to see you again.'

I was doing so well that my episode of illness was just that: part of my story to be indexed when I had enough years, chapters and disasters to form a tale of a life well lived. Disaster, bravery, combat and triumph makes a neat arc and satisfying story. The narrative constructed for me, in which I colluded, was that I had triumphed and defeated death. Now normality was enforced.

'Goodbye then,' said the surgeon who had saved me from death and knew what my brain looked like.

✠

'Let the little children come to me; do not stop them; for it is to such as these that the kingdom of God belongs.'

Mark 10.14

Children appear quite a lot in the Gospels. They never speak; almost every child is presented to Jesus by their parents, who are desperate for him to heal them. Children's innocence and vulnerability enflesh God's new Way that Jesus was forging. This Way is a path towards God's kingdom of heaven where weakness rather than strength are prized, where wisdom is not learned by rules but by the experience of suffering and need. We are invited to walk this Way. Jesus prefers foolishness, which is not naughtiness nor ignorance – it is more a sense of unknowing, of opting out of the delusional race to success. He makes it very clear. Like a compassionate mother sensing a child's danger or discomfort, Jesus pays attention, and draws attention to children.

Death and dire illness were ubiquitous at the moment when God was made flesh in Jesus, the child. Many people were demonized for their illness because it was seen as a sign of generational wrongdoing. The sense of injustice and outrage at a child's pain or death was probably not felt less then it is now, although of course, death was a very familiar part of life. We don't live among death now, we can go through life without hearing a last breath or seeing a corpse. But the death or grave illness of a child always disrupts and disorders time and expectations.

✠

I live close to Great Ormond Street Hospital in London. At any time of day or night there are parents at the entrance, nervously drawing in nicotine, whispering or crying into their phones, rubbing their eyes, exhausted. I always wonder which ward their children are in, what's wrong; and I always think of my parents waiting for me to wake up.

Parents' innocence is lost after a serious illness of a child. Their dream of perfection, of the natural order of life running smoothly, is shattered. Just like every other soon-to-be parent, the nightmare that something might go wrong with their child arrives with the first signs of pregnancy. So when illness does break out, this nightmare is lived in horrific reality. There is little a parent can do but watch and wait, try to get some sleep, and find a hand to hold.

Jesus' affection for children is a sign to us all. Every one of us is a vulnerable child after all. Children are reminders of our own fragility and their illnesses are a reminder of our mortality. Jesus' particular relationship with children magnifies for us God's tenderness. His actions teach us how to be tender towards each other. We are people, not unlike newborn children, who need others to touch and talk and play with us. We all were once in Eden, placed alongside one another to learn what it means to be human, and to be the object of God's delight.

The death of a child is unthinkable to most of us, but it is a reality for some. Death can easily feel remote, unnatural or even unreal for those who have never had a serious illness or loved someone who has been very sick. We want our bodies to remain in Eden but we have to leave; we can't stay safe and perfect and unharmed. We will all die and return to dust. Babies, children, teenagers, parents, elderly and very old people, ancient people.

Earth to earth, ashes to ashes, dust to dust.

The Wilderness

When Adam and Eve tried to gain equality with their creator and ate from the tree of knowledge of good and evil, they suddenly felt naked. Of course, they had been completely naked before, but their disobedience and pride made them feel judged and self-conscious. Delight in their own bodies and the body of another became difficult to recreate because they weren't able let go and make themselves vulnerable. Covering their nakedness and hiding was their instant response. Their bodies became a burden, a danger zone, something to tame and endlessly control. This may be reminiscent of adolescence when we had to painfully negotiate what our own bodies meant and what they could do and be.

✠

'This is my body.' We can say this to ourselves, looking straight into the mirror. Naked, we can say it to the person we love. Saying it can feel like an admission of shame, or an offering to be thankful for. Many of us shy away from our bodies, keeping them at bay; others spend lots of time and money controlling them. Inarguably, we do need to pay attention and respect them, responding to pain, being mindful of what we eat and so on. But we often presume that we are the masters of our bodies, which must be bound into submission. Plastic surgery can try and fight the power of decay but not for ever. It's not easy to learn to accept that our bodies will not always function effortlessly as the years inevitably pass. Ailments are viewed as frustrating inconveniences or a sign of failure of command and authority. We blame our feet for making it difficult to walk, as if they don't belong to us. We start to resent our bodies and turn them into an 'other', so that, if we dare look straight into the mirror we prefer to say, 'This can't be my body.' We may rarely or never confidently present our bodies to a person we desire for fear that they will not accept us.

'Get well soon.' It is a kind sentiment but it can also be a threat to someone who has been ill for some time. What does being well mean? How do we understand chronic illness? We long for normality and ease, and yearn for that Eden time when we didn't ever have to worry, or even think about our bodies, but the myth exists because it captures the frustration we feel and the weakness we must accept when we become adults.

This is My Body?

When a sudden illness occurs we begin to realize that we have taken our bodies for granted. In some ways our bodies are our servants. Our hands open jam jars, thumbs and fingers fasten bras, feet press the peddle on the accelerator. But when pain arises we are slowed down and forced to ask our bodies to do something for us – sometimes pleading for cooperation and negotiating peace. We could think of illness as an experience of being forced into the wilderness where our bodies threaten to be not just a stranger, but a dangerous and unpredictable enemy. Our bodies, our environment and our entire world view is shaken. We are abandoned into chaos.

When illness comes suddenly the outside world is frozen out. A load of wet laundry is rotting; the MOT just happened to run out that day; a dentist appointment is missed; a manager is wondering what has happened to her employee who is never normally late, never off work. Everything, everyone, has to wait.

Our bodies, unsheathed and bare, speak for us now. Our sick body seems to offer itself as we lie, trolleyed to a doctors' workshop, to those whose vocation is fulfilled by a fascination for our bodies. In an operating theatre, an assessment cubicle, a radiography room, another wounded body is revealed: a new and exciting puzzle, an original work of art, a specimen of wonder and awe, a threat, a faulty system, a treat, a tragedy. So while we must enter into a wilderness when we become ill, it might be worth recognizing that for the medical profession our bodies may be a rich, exciting jungle.

But for us it is a wilderness. We are lost; without familiar comforts, landmarks, signpost or guides. Safety, ideals and all that we have created and constructed to curate safety and security have collapsed. Our broken-down bodies have not only become chaotic, they have moved into an unfamiliar and not at all exotic zone.

A wilderness is a place of exposure. It is an environment of threat and uncertainty. No one really likes to be out of control. Powerlessness strips us of status: education, wealth, age and beauty have no currency when illness strikes. When the comforts and illusions of status are removed, the world can feel more hostile. Illness can be a great leveller.

The hospital bed we are rolled on to, even if it is only for a short time, can be a hostile place. The curtains closed for our privacy around us can be easily opened by people we have never seen before who speak in words and numbers that are hard to understand. Uniforms and titles point to nowhere beyond the hospital; the food offered is nothing like home; our bodies' rhythms and routines that were once safe taboos become public.

Sounds, moans and cries from other beds where people lie marooned sound out a universal language: pain. Body parts rarely exposed to the light or to others are touched and tested by confident explorers. Our bodies turn into findings, hoards and specimens; parts of us are taken away as data to make experiments. In the wilderness, we are no longer our own possession. We can't be, or else we won't survive.

For most of us the wilderness is probably viewed as 'elsewhere', but our own bodies can become a wilderness that we carry around with us. We are expelled from an innocent garden of complacent familiarity and security into a foreign land. We can feel trapped in it.

Beyond the wilderness of our sickbed the world continues in its predictable and fantastic ways. The delicate objects we treasured, the sophisticated predilections, petty comforts and play are absent. We have been banished. And beauty: beauty once everywhere now is nowhere.

A New Way

John the Baptist, the last in the line of Old Testament prophets, is the one called by God to prepare the way for Jesus. John, in preparation for fulfilling his vocation, choses to inhabit a hostile wilderness. It is a harsh life without comforts: a land of locusts, not milk and honey. He is pared down and set apart.

Mark's Gospel, which was the first of the four Gospels to be written, doesn't begin with Jesus. Instead, Mark quotes the urgent cries of the prophet Isaiah who foresees one who would step out of the wilderness of preparation, into a wilderness of despair and disorientation.

'See, I am sending my messenger ahead of you,
who will prepare your way;
the voice of one crying out in the wilderness:
"Prepare the way of the Lord,
make his paths straight."'

Mark 1.1-3

Zechariah's own prophetic song describes his son John's task: to clear away some of the chaotic and destructive patterns of living. He outlines the thrust of Jesus' saving work using the metaphor of a sun rising that would dispel the disorientating and pervasive darkness. Jesus will be like the first rays at dawn shedding light on those who are lost in their own wilderness. Zechariah foresees a time when death is not always a terrifying threat. It will be a bright new way of peace for us to walk in.

'And you, child, will be called the prophet of the Most High;
for you will go before the Lord to prepare his ways,
to give knowledge of salvation to his people
by the forgiveness of their sins.
By the tender mercy of our God,
the dawn from on high will break upon us,
to give light to those who sit in darkness and in the shadow of death,
to guide our feet into the way of peace.'

Luke 1.76-79

John goes into the severe desert and makes himself vulnerable and powerless. He has to experience darkness and loss before he can be a witness to Jesus who is the one who will bring light and liberate the world from its own self-imposed chaos. After 40 days in the punishing desert John is emboldened and enters into the public square claiming loudly that although they may not see it, they are living in a dark wilderness.

'The one who is more powerful than I is coming after me.'

Mark 1.7

Is *this* My Body?

The loss of innocence that some of us feel when we go through a severe or sudden illness is rarely easy to accept at first. Some people never admit their disappointment or shame and can't bear to recognize how changed they feel by their experience. There is therefore no journey to go on if shame and shock sits so deep and shakes us so much that it feels unbearable to even begin to imagine any improvement and recovery. Perhaps some people think that their body is a possession that has been unexpectedly snatched away and they are now completely bereft as though they are body-less and powerless. Unwillingness to accept what illness is doing to us can prevent any progress. If this is the case the journey out of the wilderness into recovery can easily become mere existence, without hope or positive change. Yet it is when we start to honestly reflect on what is happening to us more deeply within our sick bodies that we may begin to trust that a tragedy could ultimately become a revelation.

'I will make a make a way in the wilderness and rivers in the desert.'

Isaiah 43.19

2

Incarnation

The brain surgeon had let me out of hospital and said I was well again and back to normal. So I was. I went back to school in time for the Christmas Carol Service, and the beginning of a new year must have helped everyone in the family feel certain that I was better now and we could simply put that terrifying episode behind us and get back to normal. My thick hair covered my scar quickly, so besides that, there was not one outward sign of illness. I was without physical proof of distress or pain. I put my roller skates back on and flew up and down the streets where I lived.

The tone at St John the Baptist's primary school in the village of Baxenden was benign and friendly. Although it was not very academic, I loved learning but I did not understand what education was and what it might be for.

Before the brain haemorrhage I was one of the four pupils chosen to be on the North-West Inter-School General Knowledge Competition team – the primary school version of *University Challenge*. We didn't win any competitions despite being very well primed by Mrs Jenkins. During ordinary English lessons five of us were set apart to read together outside the classroom as our reading skills were more advanced than the rest of the class. One other pupil and I did our maths work outside the classroom on a landing, at our own fast pace. There was rarely any homework and learning often meant dull comprehension exercises in desiccated 1970s textbooks. Girls studied needlework while the boys played football. I enjoyed sewing and reached the doll-making level. I created a nurse with her own uniform and long blonde hair with a cap.

We moved house before I started at Hollins High School. Our new home was as small as the previous one, and as the youngest child there was no discussion about who would get the box room. My parents bought me a desk and my dad assembled and installed it in the attic, transforming the loft into a private study for me in preparation for my new big school.

Smart in my new – but ugly – apple and bottle-green uniform, I bounced along to my new form. There was a boy there with a fat broken nose and chest puffed out with contempt and bravado, who very quickly won the title of 'Cock o't Boyz' of the first year which – in Accrington at least – meant that he was the toughest, scariest and strongest pupil of our year. Within a week I challenged him to an arm wrestle and won.

Hollins comprehensive school was quite small – with 300 pupils – and very mixed. Many of the pupils came from council estates or the dark Victorian terraces in and around Accrington, a wet and increasingly poor town as each cotton mill closed its doors. Many pupils were Bangladeshi with little or no English. My mum was a primary school teacher in the most deprived area in Accrington and some of her pupils progressed to Hollins. The rich students from my primary school went to private secondary schools, whisked away to wealthy towns by minibus, wearing lavish purple uniforms and straw hats. Accrington Grammar closed down in 1975, the year I was born. My sister and I went to Hollins simply because it was a 10-minute walk from home; it seemed absurd to even contemplate going anywhere else. There was no sixth form and hardly anyone went to university. In fact, I knew no one who had been to university except for one of my mother's colleagues.

At the start of the school year, after two weeks of unobtrusive observation followed by tests, we were slotted into streams. I was not put in the top set; the humiliation felt worse than a pain in my head. I begged my mum to speak to the Head of Lower School – a PE teacher. Never a pushy parent, she acquiesced and met him but she was told that my test results just weren't good enough. I never used my desk in the attic and if I was ever given the odd bit of homework I did it lying in bed.

No one linked this unanticipated result with my stint in hospital less than a year earlier. I had survived; my body had been fixed, the damaging blood flow halted. The fight against my own flesh to survive was well won; I was a roller-skating miracle. It was enough simply to be thankful.

God in Flesh and Blood

And the Word became flesh and lived among us.

John 1.14

Christian faith is rooted in the celebration of human flesh. Many people may find this proposal unnerving, and in many ways it is. It appears too good to be true that God became one of us; it seems to diminish God's greatness. We are possessed by the need to create purity and order so we construct a shiny but vacuous god in that image, often in the form of success, ease and money. But God became flesh, and wounds inflicted on his body killed him.

Jesus is baptized by John in the River Jordan. In Mark's Gospel this announces the beginning of Jesus' public life and ministry. It is at this moment when the nature of God begins to be revealed in a new and surprising manner. First we learn that God is Trinity: God the Father reveals the Son, and the Holy Spirit descends upon him. Other explicit signs of new ways of knowing God abound for those who are able to watch and make connections for themselves and with each other.

In John's Gospel we are told that the Word is made flesh. Word is the English translation of the Greek word *logos*, which can be understood as wisdom, truth, a rational and universal principle. The divine *logos*, which belongs to God and is God, generously participates in human life in the person of his Son, Jesus. It is crucial to recognize that Jesus first reveals God by being pushed under muddy water by John – the unconventional religious man fresh from the wilderness. It is not pretty. Jesus who is claimed to be the Son of God allows himself to be sullied, acted upon and shamed. God participates in chaos. It is an extraordinary claim.

God's revelations through Jesus the Son only come to be fully recognized following his death and resurrection. Similarly, it is sometimes only after experiencing a severe illness that our bodies, our selves, begin to take on new identities. Our bodies can sometimes feel as though they have failed us, but if we wait and watch like those who waited following Jesus' crucifixion, we may see that our bodies can become sources of transformations. We need to be patient and watchful because these qualities do not come easily, especially when we are in agony, or become obsessed that we may soon die.

It is at the beginning and end of Christ's life where we cannot fail to see the suffering and loss of autonomy that Jesus willingly embraced. This seems very different from the claim we hear in the last book of the Bible, the book of Revelation, that Jesus is the beginning and the end – the Alpha and Omega – of the entire cosmic creation. The contrast is not necessarily easy to hold together, but it is at the very heart of Christianity.

Jesus' physical presence points at every turn in the New Testament to the messy reality of human suffering. Jesus does not run away from pain and trauma. So when we are ill or recovering we can begin to see our progression as a walk in the Way of recovery with Christ. We do not need to try to engineer a scar-free, drug-free, and pain-free body.

Then Jesus was led up by the Spirit into the wilderness to be tempted by the devil.

Matthew 4.1

The Desert

Immediately after his baptism Jesus enters the desert. Jesus' flight from the lush riverbanks to the arid desert reveals so much to us about how his body participates in our physical distress and suffering. Those who are experiencing physical discomfort may take comfort in Jesus' solitary experience in the desert. God subjects himself to further humiliation through his 40-day sojourn in the desert. Such vulnerability may be shocking to many, but this is how and who God is. Jesus surrenders to God the creator.

Thinking about Jesus' 40-day defenceless subjection to hardship may help us to see the initial experiences of suffering bodies, or the first stage of recovery, as a period in the desert.

The devil is like a parasite, pushing and plotting for Jesus to assume control and power. In the creation myth Eve is tricked by a snake and chooses to eat the apple through greed, innocence, naivety. Throughout Jesus' desert pilgrimage he refuses each test the devil proposes. Jesus becomes an Israelite wandering hungrily in the desert but he remains obedient to the will of the Father. Like Elijah in the desert (1 Kings 19.4–9) he doesn't cry out for manna, even though Matthew's description of Jesus' trials was clearly physically testing: 'And he was famished' (Matthew 4.2). This description of Jesus' physical need foreshadows Jesus' desperate cry, 'I am thirsty', at the crucifixion (John 19.28). He undergoes this testing to prove his resistance to autonomy and ease. We learn through Christ that God, whose nature is 'I offer you', also becomes 'I need you'.

The idea of Jesus' willingness to participate in weak human flesh could not be clearer. For those of us whose life feels fragile and those who sense that they have been made powerless, Jesus' life-threatening experience in the desert may become a vital clue towards understanding how or why Christianity has something to offer to those who are in physical or psychological pain.

> Because he himself was tested by what he suffered, he is able to help those who are being tested.
>
> Hebrews 2.18

✠

There are very few places to hide in the desert. Its vast and desolate space can feel terrifying. Extremes of light and dark, heat and cold are brutal. In a desert place we are exposed and we can create very few boundaries around us for protection. We can take nothing for granted, and if we are unprepared it is very easy to perish. A lack of water simply means the lack of life. In the desert we are laid bare; we become tiny fragile lives between the endless sand and cloudless sky.

When we are suffering, once the shock has begun to subside, we need to move on in our pilgrimage from the chaotic disorientation of the wilderness to the stark exposure of the desert. This could be physical or mental suffering; it can be the hospital ward, the rehabilitation centre, our front room. It can also be created in our minds. But we need to be there for a while. It is a place we have to enter into even though it may feel terrifying or absurd. We need to learn that being 'somewhere else' will not necessarily make everything better straight away. This desert experience is a time and a place of contemplation about what has happened and is happening to us. Most of this must be done alone. There will be people alongside us on our journey later. Now is not a time to ask for platitudes and empty reassurances. Perhaps your body will never recover fully. Perhaps everything about your life will have to change; it changed already when the pain struck. This is not familiar territory. We are not surrounded by accrued possessions, symbols of success and idols of specialness here. Our body may suddenly look or feel like a foreign land to ourselves.

In the desert we have to respect our body's needs and be sensitive to its limitations. In the desert pride can kill. Although it is not a place to stay in for ever, a period of time in the desert is necessary. The desert is a place to wait and stop in order to move forward towards recovery. It is not a time to prepare to be useful in the world again. To get through this we must surrender power and independence. Recovering from illness is not annual leave, it is hard work.

In John Clare's poem, 'Noon', we are offered a lesson in watching, stillness and cherishing God's creation through our human senses. This is an English Eden.

Noon
The mid-day hour of twelve the clock counts o'er,
A sultry stillness lulls the air asleep;
The very buzz of flies is heard no more,
Nor faintest wrinkles o'er the waters creep.
Like one large sheet of glass the waters shine,
Reflecting on their face the burnt sunbeam:
The very fish their sporting play decline,
Seeking the willow-shadows 'side the stream.

And, where the hawthorn branches o'er the pool,
The little bird, forsaking song and nest,
Flutters on dripping twigs his limbs to cool,
And splashes in the stream his burning breast.
O, free from thunder, for a sudden shower,
To cherish nature in this noon-day hour!

John Clare

Yet our time in the desert is not like this work of observation and cherishing the present moment. The noonday hour in the desert is the most harmful. There is a time and a place for revelling safely in God's world; if we allow ourselves time and nurture a sense of hope we will get there. John Clare's poem is a reminder that God invites and encourages us to stop, wait and watch. We are shown here the value of rest and the pleasure of observation. The sonnet is a hymn of praise to the glory of God's creation. By a cool pool on a summer's day nature is safe, reassuring and predictable with the flowering hawthorn and the sporting fish. In this poem the sun is not damaging us; the air is still; we want to stay for a while; why would we want to rush off? John Clare has created a lush and intimate paradise where we are reminded of the power of pausing and the pleasure of abundance. This experience is by no means ours yet. At this stage we have to lay ourselves bare and resist the urge to escape somewhere soothing and leafy. But it will come in its own way; just not yet.

✠

It would have been simpler if something very physical and visible had happened to me. If I had lost a leg and rolled up to my new school in a wheelchair, adjustments would have been made to make my life simpler, more comfortable and fairer. Helpers may have been sent and equipment provided because doctors would have pronounced me disabled. We could have got a blue badge for the car warning everyone that someone with weaknesses of one kind or another was approaching and a parking place was required right next to the supermarket entrance. That blue disabled symbol – a semi-abstract image of a white man in a wheelchair – would have become an icon preceding me wherever I went.

I had lost a portion of my peripheral vision after my brain haemorrhage but I hardly noticed it. Or did I ignore it? No doctor tested it, nothin g was explained, but the written page must have looked squeezed and the lines of words uneven. No one could see *for me*, and my eyes were not outwardly and visibly harmed because the damage done was hidden in my brain. I was brain damaged but they never told me that. Those two words together were never spoken. I presumed that only people who couldn't speak or walk or think could be brain damaged. I believed the neurosurgeon, Mr. R. A. C. Jones, sent me home fixed and neatly finished.

To access a brain the skull has to be drilled open and a portion of the cranium is taken away. A brain is only exposed to light and air as a last resort. Every micro-millimetre of the brain contains a thousand functions so each cell tampered with risks ruin. It is the powerhouse of a body's vital functions but its intricate delicacy must make every neurosurgeon repeatedly marvel at its mysteriousness.

I have seen magnetic resonance images of my brain and there is a dark, watery, egg-shaped absence in the lower side of the right hemisphere. I have never seen an exposed brain; when I see medical procedures on television I cry instantly and turn away, squeamish.

Brains have the slippery consistency of jelly but the grandiose complexity of a cathedral. When a brain surgeon operates it is as though she is a musician reading a score as she inspects it through microscopic binoculars. At each moment she must interpret the brain before her and visualize the effect her intervention may have on the rest of the body and the rest of the person's life. Each touch can create catastrophic damage. If the patient survives the surgery, then any further damage done is only revealed once they are woken up. Perhaps he will be paralysed; he may be blind, or unable to speak. Sometimes brain surgery is carried out under local anaesthetic. The patient is talked to and tested while the brain is treated so that the surgeon has concrete proof of how beneficial it is to intervene. Some surgical procedures inevitably create harm, but the damage done may not be as dramatic or immediately obvious when the patient wakes up. She may even be able to say who the prime minister is while she takes a sip of hospital tea.

There are many forms of acquired brain injuries. In fact, each brain injury is often strange, and always unique. It is easier to gauge the damage done when the brain is affected at an older age because there is a longer 'then' to compare with 'now'. Younger brains are more plastic and ruptures tend to repair more easily – but that's not always the case. Some damage is not reparable. Brain damage can affect the long- and short-term memory in many different ways. The millions of connections the brain makes may be interrupted so thinking can be muffled and clogged up. The everyday things we do, such as stirring soup in a pan while talking about tomorrow's weather forecast, may no longer be possible. Multitasking, also known as executive functioning, disproportionately taxes damaged brains. Most people with damaged brains want, or need, to live *slower, gentler lives.*

Once a brain has been interfered with words can become impossible to locate and possess. Sometimes when I am talking, a word I want to use seems to swim away. I know it has been there once, I can see its tail because 99 per cent of the time I can correctly say what letter the word begins with. The whole word is elusive. I find facts and instructions overwhelming and difficult to digest. Visual experiences can be hard to recall too. Someone recently told me that they had been thinking about a conversation we had in Dublin. Did I go to Dublin? Memories and past events, not only those that happened long ago, lurk behind high fences with only a few holes or cracks in them. Information such as lists, numbers and dates can be uncontainable and virtually impossible to connect. Concentration tends to be extremely difficult because damaged brains are like incorrectly wired circuits with a low and irreplaceable battery. *Flow,* that plastic flash that is sparked a billion times over and set alight in the brain, cannot so easily be let loose to ignite a person's whole being when the brain has been tampered with.

Emotions and personalities can also be changed following brain surgery. What we do, who we are and how we are, sit precariously within our skull. Even more strangely perhaps, we can become 'emotionally labile', which means that we may swing too quickly between emotional states. Disinhibition, anger and even increased libido can all be new and sometimes unwelcome facets of a person's identity following damage to the brain. Some things are added and some are taken away.

✠

I recently I had a neuropsychological test for the first time. For over three hours a young, friendly neuropsychologist showed me pictures, asked me to repeat words, draw lines and remember images. The results were startling. The tests are calibrated using 300 healthy people of all ages. My visual recall was a dismal 10th percentile, as was my ability to remember facts and words. I discovered that my visio-spatial reasoning (such as doing a jigsaw puzzle) was well below average, and my perceptual ability (interpreting two-dimensional representations of three-dimensional objects) and executive functioning (doing more than one thing at a time), were also below average. Word-finding and language fluency was low too. My language comprehension was described as simply 'intact'. The only very pleasing high score was in the 'intellectual functioning' (making connections with ideas and concepts) category; I scored in the 99th percentile of the population. To read this report was like being given the map and clues to a treasure hunt. To receive a letter from the consultant neuropsychologist saying that I have very superior intellectual ability was like winning the lottery.

I had that test when I was 37. I was 11 years old when Mr R. A. C. Jones first cut into my head to stem bleeding arteries with a spring-loaded titanium clip.

Walking the Desert Way

The desert is a pared-down existence. We have to adapt to it because it will not adapt to us. Recovery is a process of making physical, mental, practical, relational and spiritual adaptations. It is hard work.

There is not much to do in the desert. The light is brutal, the sand is abrasive There is nothing to choose; safety and security is only a mirage and it cannot be purchased; there is only the call to be. We can't rush off to normality now that our brains are changed. There is no normality after a serious illness anyway. We can't escape it, we can't rush back to the garden of Eden where our bodies obediently enjoyed life for us.

A number of fourth-century Christians who became known as the 'desert fathers and mothers' did not flee the fertile banks of the Nile to the harsh Egyptian deserts in order to escape reality. Instead, they chose to live in the desert in order to inhabit themselves more fully. They chose to be there and to do nothing. With extremes of space and silence, and the absence of cover and company, they learned to be comfortable in their own skin, with their bodies. This required radical honesty and it was their quest for honesty that led them to this barren landscape. They didn't only see it as a test, but as an opportunity too. They weren't discovering themselves by being offered choices. Instead, they were discovering themselves by opening their hearts and finding new words and ways to understand themselves. They sat in the shadow of stones listening to the silence and learning to hear God's inspiration breathing through the windy landscape. They didn't run for cover. They didn't go to the desert as a self-imposed punishment, although there is no denying that this was an extreme choice. By making themselves vulnerable they hoped to be transformed to a more intimate encounter with God.

✠

When our bodies are sick there is a lot of waiting to be done, which can be frustrating and infuriating. For some people a time of illness may be the first time they experience a sense of powerlessness. It can be easy to presume that this kind of powerlessness through illness is like mistakenly finding ourselves in the longest, slowest queue in the supermarket. But rage at our loss of power slows our recovery and traumatizes us even more. Running back to find familiarity can be futile; fighting weakness with wrongly assumed strength can hurt. Notions of strength and weakness when we are ill are very different now. Strength and weakness begin to take on new and bewildering meanings. In the early stages of illness or recovery we must learn how to respect the heart, to be quiet so we can hear it and so honour the sound it is making and the work it is doing. Here we may begin to learn to accept that God is in there with us, especially in the waves of impatience and impotence. We tend to live disembodied fantasies, giving preference to our minds over our matter, so it can be terrifying to begin to understand how the purpose and the potential of our bodies can suddenly be the dictators of our destiny.

Extended or sudden exposure to apparently empty time and empty space can feel like a boring void, but the desert is the place to learn who we are becoming. Layers of defence are sloughed off at a time when our bodies are forced into stillness. We can use this time as part of our journey, however paradoxical this may seem. The desert landscape can be a place where despair is embraced and even lived out. A desert place need not be a place of ennui, rather, it may become an imagined landscape for us to experience and confront our new bodies. New bodies can tell fresh and startling truths – but we need to be still and alone in order to attend to them.

Time in the desert may be long, it may only be brief, but it should not be rushed over. It will take as long as it takes. It is not easy to test recovery. We must question not, 'Who am I?' but, 'What is happening in me?' In the desert the mind and the body must cooperate. The emptiness of the desert gives us time to encourage the mind and body to greet each other, perhaps for the first time. This is the place where we begin to dismantle old defences and delve beneath the surface of our body to hear what may be speaking in its depths. The silent desert is a place to begin to learn to listen and begin to find new words and new ways of making sense of our experience.

This making sense can only be done with periods of time in silence and solitude. No one else possesses our body, even though it may feel suddenly owned by those around us, such as the bedside-nurses checking and noting, or doctors inspecting. The desert is a place where we must conform in order for it to be a place of radical but perhaps uncomfortable truth-telling.

Most church services begin in the west, in the nave. The congregation gathers with the baptismal font behind them. They may have dipped their finger in a stoop or bowl of blessed water by the great open door and wet a cross on their foreheads, reminding them of their baptism. As the service begins the people are 'collected' by a prayer said by the priest and then called to repentance. At every Eucharist the people who have come to worship God are called to change and be changed. Still with a damp forehead, the congregation is invited to turn away for a while from the chaos and mess and symbolic dimness of the west to face east where light always begins. This shift from darkness to light is a moment of transformation and turning towards light where we remember again that we are invited to come closer to Christ and even become like him. We need to get closer, moving away from the west, going east towards the altar, facing Jerusalem where Christ died. We can learn that by accepting vulnerability we will begin to convert towards God. *To convert* originally means 'to turn'. Conversion towards God's Way by repentance is not a shaming punishment. We are not washed clean by an angry parent wiping our mouth after being caught gorging on forbidden chocolate. God's tender mercy must be experienced in the heart; it cannot be learned by the head alone.

Almighty God,
whose Son Jesus Christ fasted 40 days in the wilderness
and was tempted as we are, yet without sin;
give us grace to discipline ourselves to your Spirit
and as you know our weakness, so may we know your power
to save.

The Collect for the first Sunday of Lent

Entering into the desert is a repeated motif in the season of Lent, which is a 40-day pilgrimage. It involves a discipline of self-denial where we strip ourselves of the fetters which hide us from God and from ourselves. Lent is an annual invitation to inwardly and outwardly unmake ourselves. But aren't we unmade as we flail in agony in an unmade, inhospitable sickbed? Surely. When we are sick we are stripped literally of clothes and metaphorically of dignity when pain incapacitates our bodies. We might think of illness as a process of unmaking. Recovery and making sense of survival requires us to hold on to that feeling of powerlessness and despair. In Lent though it is done intentionally each year. Being stripped down in sickness can be cruel and both emotionally and psychologically devastating. If we intend to make sense of illness by going along a journey, this means of transformation is best described as a Way with God first forged by Christ in the desert. We are surviving but we must also resist the temptation to presume that all is well, all is normal again and victory has been won.

Lent
Lent is a tree without blossom, without leaf
Barer than blackthorn in its winter sleep
All unadorned. Unlike Christmas which decrees
The setting-up, the dressing-up of trees,
Lent is a taking down, a stripping bare,
A starkness after all has been withdrawn
Of surplus and superfluous,
Leaving no hiding-place, only an emptiness
Between black branches, a most precious space
Before the leaf, before the time of flowers;
Lest we should see only the leaf, the flower,
Lest we should miss the stars.

Jean M. Watt

In Jean Watt's poem the sight of stars is an incentive, giving meaning and purpose to the hassle of stripping down our lives. But it is difficult, if not impossible when we are sick, to be so certain of what our future will look like. If we are very ill, 40 days is unlikely to be enough time to make new sense of our debilitated bodies, which may feel taken down and forgotten. Recovery often takes much longer than we expect and any improvement may not even be easy to detect. Our bodies are unreliable and unpredictable. Recovery has no finish line to triumphantly break through.

It is important to remember that the Word made flesh who enters the desert is not an abstract idea. It is Jesus Christ; it is our stricken body. Illness changes our incarnation. Time spent crossing the desert can be a time when we may begin to think again about our own flesh – our incarnation. Even though our flesh may create humiliation for us for a time, we can hold fast to the reality that God's flesh was humiliated before ours. As we cross the desert we can begin to learn what our new calling might be. We should not rush. Discovering the physical, emotional and psychological trauma inflicted on our bodies is part of this journey.

3

Identity

When I was 14 I had a boyfriend called John. We had spent late Friday afternoon 'down the lines' as we called it, along the straight, flat path paved by the disused railway. As we walked we talked about what we would do when we left school and where we could go in the summer holidays which were not far off. John was about two years older and about to take his GCSEs. He intended to study dance and drama. He went back to his home and I to mine and we agreed to meet up the next day.

It was warm for early May and still light when I went to bed. But it was dark, towards midnight, when I switched off the light. Just as I was about to fall asleep I felt a pain that was as sharp as an axe cracking a cleavage – not into my skull, though that felt shattered too – but inside my head, gouging out my brain, slicing it, making it instantly seethe, ooze and choke blood. I saw lights in the darkness and flashes of darkness that were the visible residues of the electrical storm in my head. I sat up, blinded in sight, by fear, and through pain. My body felt loaded and I strained to get out of bed.

'I'm having a brain haemorrhage,' I announced to my sleeping parents in the dark room next door. It was a statement of fact, not conjecture. I half jumped, half fell on to their bed just as they both jumped out of it, rushing towards me. They knew I was right.

'All right, Jen. All right,' said my dad as he put his hand on my shoulder. I felt my mum rush beside me and heard her on the phone, calling for an ambulance, not a doctor like last time. I vomited all over the duvet and slumped and smeared my long mane of hair in it. I groaned out the pain through my throat. My mum returned to the bedside but did not turn on the light.

Very soon, an encroaching blackness highjacked my vision from its peripheries. I went still, not sleeping, but not dead.

The ambulance took me to a small local hospital. Friday night, 2 a.m. The on-call junior doctors were tired and probably envious of their friends' sleep and freedom, and longed for the morning. Dozing, they insisted to my parents that it would be best to wait for the morning when a senior doctor would be there.

'We know what it is,' my mum and dad urged, but the doctors resisted their insight.

'Are you going to let our daughter die?' my dad asked. 'She'll die if you don't take her to the neurologist. This isn't a bad head-ache. Our daughter is dying.'

Dawn was breaking when an ambulance unloaded me and my parents at a hospital in Salford, not far from the children's unit where my skull was opened for the first time, less than four years earlier.

The same surgeon was called in, Mr R. A. C. Jones. My scarred brain and the congenitally malformed cells were not as efficiently controlled as he had wished. It is not unusual for brain malfor-mations such as mine to bleed again, but this bleed was much more extensive than the first. My skull was reopened and the bleeding, clotted brain was clipped shut again. A bigger hole was made; there were more cells drowning in blood and damaging even more of my brain. My head was stitched back up exactly in the same spot, leaving only one thick scar, a poor consolation for two battles.

Again they waited to see if I would wake up, or who would wake up. Everybody waited again.

My eyes were sealed with grey chalky paste but I gradually real-ized that I saw light beyond this veil. My mouth was caked with dry powdered saliva, spiked by chemicals, spread by instruments blowing, sucking, flowing, saving. Water was being stirred up, something was heard before it was felt. Warm liquid was being sponged on to my right foot.

'Hello, Jennie.' The voice was shiny. 'Nice to see ya.' She moved to the top of the bed and her face matched the smiling tone and timbre of her speech.

'Just giving you a wash, lovey.' More splash, and the smell of Scottish ferns. Then warm strokes along my arms. 'There we go,' she whispered. 'Nice and clean.' She travelled around the side of the bed and began sponging my chest. I turned away from her. My mother and father were beside me. Naked, and fourteen years old, I was surrounded. My mother's head rested on my father's shoulder, her face folded into frowns. At first, only my dad's stubbly chin was visible. His blank look faced the ceiling with his mouth open wide as if in shock and supplication at once. His breath rasped. Absent at my miracle awakening, as longed for as at birth, a stranger on the nightshift witnessed it. Covered up, retucked in, I felt her breath, 'Well done, kid.'

I woke up half-blind. Literally, I saw half the world exactly, in both eyes, so the left half of the world had vanished. Half my body was stuck stiff. The left side was completely paralysed; it is a condition called *hemiparesis*. It was like a stroke: precisely half my body was damaged as though a vertical line had been drawn right through the middle of me. I felt completely numb; my left arm and leg were like wood, not teenage flesh alive with energy and desire.

My mouth worked though, and I could speak. I knew who the prime minister was (it was still Margaret Thatcher) so cognitive functions had not completely collapsed. I knew where I was too but there were no animal cartoons on the ceiling. At fourteen I was viewed as an adult, so I was housed in Hope Hospital, Salford. I was brave again. And so were my parents, but they were weary and terrified; but thankful, very thankful.

My parents stayed beside me. John also came every day, almost abandoning his exams, patiently sitting beside my bedside while I slept. My sister was in the same class as he and also preparing to sit exams. She went to stay with friends and visited when she could. And again, my faithful grandparents visited every day.

Two bouncy physiotherapists, a man and a woman, arrived at my bedside each morning to try and relay neural pathways in my brain so that I would gain sensation in my limbs. They lifted up my stone leg, pulled it round, bent my toes and circled my foot. When I was helped out of a wheelchair I hobbled like a frail, fall-prone elderly woman. I was held by the hand the way toddlers are when they begin to take their first steps. When I was ready to sit up, John and I developed a way of encouraging my stiff fingers to smooth out. We copied the hand movements in the video of 'Rhythm Nation' by Janet Jackson. The slick hand gestures of the dancers emancipated me. I am left-handed. I will never be a quick typist because the fingers on my left hand are not as lithe as those on my right. My handwriting is poor. I have to consciously 'think' in order to move my little and ring fingers; they feel like faulty parts of machinery that cannot be oiled, fixed or replaced. It is still difficult for me to tell hot water from cold; the circulation in my left limbs is sluggish, and they easily turn blue in the winter.

I had another angiogram so that the neurologists could see whether the new clips in my brain were securely fitted. Another bleed might kill me: third time unlucky? Undoubtedly more cautious now, the doctors were not satisfied that the nest of mangled blood vessels was as stable as they liked. I remember Mr Jones sitting on the end of my bed, and a short American visiting neurologist standing beside him. They both looked very serious. I sensed their nervousness but perhaps it was pity, or sorrow, or even regret. They tried to explain what they had seen in the scan. Mr Jones struggled to find words he thought would suit me. He suggested further treatment: embolization, which is a procedure to block malformed arteries, preventing them from leaking and bleeding again.

Before I was sedated, a young female doctor sat beside my waist in the operating theatre. She leaned towards me and said, 'Jennie, I know this might be uncomfortable for you but I'm going to have to shave your pubic hair.'

I bit my lip, closed my eyes and must have only nodded my consent. I was not anaesthetized completely so the theatre was indeed a macabre show. I was at once the act and the audience. After the pubic area was shaved clean surgical glue was inserted into my groin using an enormous syringe. I felt it coursing up my body, arrive at the back of my neck, and heard it sucking, brainward, behind my right ear. I could hear it squish. The sounds have stuck in my memory but the humiliation has nearly faded.

My parents later told me that my face was green when I was wheeled back to the ward. When the neurologist returned with

Mr Jones they did not sit at my bed, but stood at the end of it and announced that the embolization hadn't worked. They sent me home.

My long hair covered my scar, and although the back of my head looked unevenly thin on one side it was not ugly or bloody. My mum took four weeks off work to look after me. I did not return to school till September. Beguilingly intelligent female home tutors arrived respectively two mornings a week for the next few months. I enjoyed talking to them, sitting at the dining room table with one, chatting on the sofa with another. I was unable to write properly though; my hand was still a gnarly club. I visited school just once to choose which GCSEs I would like to study in September. I sat in the deputy head teacher's office for 20 minutes and ticked my choices. I was sent away with a thin and fearful smile. My parents cancelled our summer holiday to Yugoslavia because the doctors said that it might be unsafe for me to fly. We went to Torquay instead. My parents told me it was called the English Riviera.

The Flight out of Egypt

'This is why I have let you live: to show you my power, and to make my name resound through all the earth.'

Exodus 9.16

The story of the exodus of the people of Israel is a key biblical narrative for Christians as well as Jews. The hardship, the struggle, the long and seemingly interminable journey, the expectation and the vulnerability that is described over and over again creates a corporate identity for the people of Israel. For many who are beginning to recover, this theme of struggling along a difficult journey towards an unknown place at a sluggish pace may sound familiar. Like the tale of the exodus of God's chosen people, our story of recovery has to be constructed, reconstructed and retold. It is a tale of becoming, which takes a long time, lots of patience and honest reflection.

Surviving an illness is a liberation of its own. Following a time of watching and waiting in the desert, we need to move forward and discover ourselves as we go. It is this next phase – a journey that begins at the point of escape from death – where we learn more about who we are. We are changed; it is a new beginning.

Understanding the nature of who we are is everyone's life's work, although strangely we often presume that we just know who we are. So much so perhaps that we rarely if ever think about it. We seem to use a rather narrow set of identifiers to explain who we are to others, and even to ourselves. Our gender and skin colour come first. Our occupation and marital status often follow. For some, the place we live comes close to the top. Children are offered as indicators and signposts of who we are. It is worth noting where we might place our faith when trying to respond to the question, 'Who are you?' In the loneliness that seems to be inevitable when we are ill, identifiers that have been acquired over the years can quickly fall away. Home, job, finances, clothes, status, beauty can all vanish without preparation. Then what are we left with?

✠

When the people of Israel are led out of Egypt they are divested of their belongings. Moses, afraid and terrified, leads a group of lost and weary people. At least they are identified as belonging to God – chosen as God's elected people. This gives the Israelites a collective identity, providing a sense of safety – however shaky. The people of Israel choose to be led. They surrender control. It is humiliating and frustrating but it is better than the confusion and trauma of slavery in a foreign land.

Trials and tests are at the heart of the Christian faith; our deep roots stem from the people of Israel. We also have to walk our way to becoming who God has ultimately called us to be. Faith is not an abstract noun, nor is it a possession; it is an activity in which a person and God encounter each other. As we pull ourselves away from the shock of the body blow of sickness towards recovery, the best way towards liberation is to recognize that God leads us and is completely present with us. Salvation belongs to those who, in relationship, cooperate with God to help draw them out of danger. Arising from our sickbed is not the only liberation to be experienced, although it may initially feel like it.

Salvation starts by entering into the trauma of shock and pain, and allowing God to do something, a new thing with us, not merely to or for us.

> What else can save us but your hand, remaking what you have made?
>
> Augustine, *Confessions*, 4.7

The fourth-century bishop and theologian Augustine's autobiography, *Confessions*, can be seen as a story of exodus. Augustine reconstructs his past from childhood to the present, noting over and over his blindness, his resistance to God and his ignorance of the loving presence of God. In retrospect Augustine recognizes that God was revealed to him in signs waiting to be interpreted. It is not a neat and orderly account of a life in the modern sense. The more he investigates his past, the more unstable his present identity and experiences become. Augustine's personal liberation begins in the moment when he hears children playing in the garden singing a song which includes the Latin words, *tolle lege*, 'pick up and read'. He picks up a Bible, opens it at random, and comes across part of Paul's letter to the Romans. It speaks to his dilemma of how he should live in order to feel fully alive.

> But where was I when I looked for you? You were there before my eyes, but I had deserted even my own self. I could not find myself, much less find you.
>
> Augustine, *Confessions*, 5.2

Augustine's salvation though self-discovery is not a one-off event. It is a process that is lived out in prayer and worship. His personal account of losing himself and being found by God is addressed to God, as in conversation. Making sense of his life is made possible by constructing and telling his own life story. It is a constant shifting process, a journey towards the heart of God. Liberation through finding God and being found by God is the leitmotif for Augustine's life, and through this he develops a deep self-awareness and gratitude.

Augustine is mindful of the precariousness of existence. He did not suffer severe physical illness but he admits that he was enamoured by vanity, power and wealth. His disease was pride, but he was tormented by an existential search for meaning. A chance moment of awareness of the reality of God led him away from his false and fettered self. His refreshed identity is rooted in his experience of God's absence and presence, of the necessity of watching and waiting attentively and patiently. His liberation to living a new way of life meant a conversion to a life praising God without end.

The Journey Out of Slavery

Identity is not simple or fixed; it is compound and fluid. Even our gender is not as concrete as many people would like to believe. Our identity is lived out in the everyday things we do, so when our lives feel hampered by poor health, we may find it terrifying to even begin to ask ourselves, 'Who am I?' or especially, 'Who am I now?' Which part of ourselves is asking the question? Who answers? Ruptures in who we think we are, and also once were, can make us long to go back to a place or time we begin to call 'before'.

✠

The people of Israel begged to return to enslavement in Egypt when conditions began to deteriorate in the wilderness.

> 'If only we had died by the hand of the LORD in the land of Egypt.'
>
> Exodus 16.3

The Israelites did not know what to expect or what to aim for, so returning to what was known – slavery – felt like a safer, more desirable option. But they knew they couldn't ever return. God promised to liberate them so they just had to listen, trust and be patient. God's chosen ones only realized how reformed they had become once their long journey had ended. For those of us struck by illness this can be a frustrating tale. There is no grand arrival, no promise of milk and honey in sight. Perfection – even normality – are fantasies we need to deconstruct and relinquish. And anyway, we are always unfinished.

'I will be with you.'

Exodus 3.12

✠

It can be tempting to look back at what we used to do, how we used to be, and effortlessly look forward to our future potential. Yet who we are in the present matters. Our identity, who we are, is a constant process of becoming. If we are to move out of the desert and make sense of our identity in the light of illness we must renegotiate ourselves. In going forward we may recognize that, as our unique self is revealed, so is a new reality of God. If we hope, God accompanies us along the Way; the two are inseparable.

God's presence and God's purpose allows us to believe that he travels alongside us as we make progress. Progress may mean less pain, better sleep, getting out of bed before noon, becoming less anxious, leaving the house or going to work. God moves us onward to a different place. This doesn't mean that we are required to wipe out all that has happened before, not least because the story of the exodus is not one of escape, but of transformation.

The Flight into Health

Then Moses said to Aaron, 'Say to the whole congregation of the Israelites, "Draw near to the LORD, for he has heard your complaining."'

Exodus 16.9

We prize independence: we want to go where we want and do what we want whenever it suits us. Independence is often seen as the goal, a great achievement to boast about, as if it is a possession gained by strength and endurance. We mould our children so that they may be self-sufficient. We mourn when elderly people require extra care. We feel ashamed when we ask for help, and apologize for our weakness.

> When my soul was embittered,
>   when I was pricked in heart,
> I was stupid and ignorant;
>   I was like a brute beast towards you.
> Nevertheless I am continually with you;
>   you hold my right hand.
> You guide me with your counsel,
>   and afterwards you will receive me with honour.
>
> Psalm 73.21–24

The lure of complete well-being is pervasive and sold as the ultimate form of salvation. Sick bodies cannot be rushed or rubbed better. Shamed by physical weakness, we may strive for strength but our bodies and brains can often feel the strain of 'too much too soon'. Others – our friends and our employers – often collude in our premature flights into health because illness is boring and inconvenient. People can react in new and strange ways; they may be afraid of offending us, or even looking at us because our weakness unsettles them. They may wish our sickness hadn't happened; it disrupts the flow of life that so much effort is put into controlling. Those who love us will want to help and many of our relationships will almost inevitably change, which can be unsettling. It may take time to admit and understand in what ways they have shifted. We have to accept and even dare to tell others that we may have to get worse before we get better. This may be uncomfortable to hear and might cause a different kind of pain or regret of its own. 'Getting better' has little to do with being back to normal. Recovery reaches far beyond a healed bone or the all-clear after cancer.

Jesus did not heal those who were sick in order to make them useful again. The various illnesses of those Jesus met caused them to be dependent on others. Some had been outcast by their communities. They were probably used to the effects their illness had on those they were dependent on, even in their family homes: 'We can't cope with your difference; spare us from our own shame we feel when we see you; we wish you were normal like us.' Bartimaeus, the blind beggar, sitting at the gate in Jericho who we meet in Mark's Gospel (Mark 10.46–52) begs Jesus for mercy twice and he is healed on the spot.

> The blind man said to him, 'My teacher, let me see again.' Jesus said to him, 'Go; your faith has made you well.' Immediately he regained his sight and followed him on the way.
>
> Mark 10.51–52

With returned sight, Bartimaeus could have gone back home immediately and reclaimed dignity for himself and his family. Instead, he follows Jesus 'along the Way' to Jerusalem where, less than a week later Jesus would be blinded by blood, sweat and pain. Bartimaeus exchanges the stigma of dependence created by illness for the stigma of failure. Bartimaeus the blind beggar, crying out for mercy, reveals remarkable insight. He knows and trusts that Jesus will be the one who sees beyond the uncomfortable vision of a scrawny blind man with a hand cupped to catch spare change. Yet repaired vision will not make Bartimaeus whole at all; it is his encounter with Jesus that transfigures his sight. Bartimaeus does not go back to his hometown to recreate normality. He goes forward, with the Son of God to an unknown destination. Rather than his renewed sight it is his experience of Jesus' love that allows Bartimaeus to walk freely with him. He has no destination; he walks along the Way beside Jesus. This is his identity now.

The Flight into Ease

> The LORD said to Moses, 'Go, leave this place, you and the people whom you have brought up out of the land of Egypt, and go to the land of which I swore to Abraham, Isaac, and Jacob, saying, "To your descendants I will give it." I will send an angel before you, and I will drive out the Canaanites, the Amorites, the Hittites, the Perizzites, the Hivites, and the Jebusites. Go up to a land flowing with milk and honey.'
>
> Exodus 33.1-3

We all have our own milk and honey place – our imagined destination where everything will be calm and safe. It is important to remember that in the book of Exodus the land of milk and honey is a metaphor for ease and comfort. It is a place where everything is done for us. Nothing is asked of us, nothing stops us from choosing and curating our own bespoke lifestyle. We feed our fantasies of entering into our land of milk and honey because, once there, we will not need to ask ourselves difficult questions about our purpose, our delusions and fears. A shimmering veneer eclipses our messy identities accumulated through experiences of disappointments, failures and losses. This land of ease forces a hazy forgetfulness. We can try to escape to this imaginary idyllic place through different means such as alcohol and anything which disembodies us. Shopping, the internet and social media take us there for a while, but if we keep trying to flee to a place of ease our traumatized body is disconnected from us.

There is no hope of transformation if we believe that nothing significant about our current situation needs to be changed. If we are stubborn in admitting our vulnerability our pretend normality will become increasingly uncomfortable and not at all easy to maintain.

✠

The German theologian Dietrich Bonhoeffer (1906–45) was imprisoned and later murdered by the Nazis for being part of the plot to assassinate Hitler. The letters written to his parents, fiancée and friends from prison reveal frank insights as he grapples with his extended incarceration. He was not ill, but his loss of freedom combined with his uncertain future may help us understand our approach to making sense of our personal fears and struggles.

He confesses that he is aware that his inner life does not match his outer self. His isolation is heightened further because his public demeanour is healthy, upbeat, even proud. He deludes himself into thinking that he is unable to find someone in prison to whom he can turn for help and empathy. He resists finding people to bring him some comfort, who can help him understand who he is becoming. His poem 'Who am I?' is an admission of fakery in the face of despair. He is trapped, exhausted and ashamed of his pretence.

Who am I?
Who am I? They often tell me
I stepped from my cell's confinement
Calmly, cheerfully, firmly,
Like a Squire from his country house.

Who am I? They often tell me
I used to speak to my warders
Freely and friendly and clearly,
As though it were mine to command.

Who am I? They also tell me
I bore the days of misfortune
Equably, smilingly, proudly,
like one accustomed to win.

Am I then really that which other men tell of?
Or am I only what I myself know of myself?
Restless and longing and sick, like a bird in a cage,
Struggling for breath, as though hands were compressing my throat,
Yearning for colours, for flowers, for the voices of birds,

Thirsting for words of kindness, for neighbourliness,
Tossing in expectations of great events,
Powerlessly trembling for friends at an infinite distance,
Weary and empty at praying, at thinking, at making,
Faint, and ready to say farewell to it all.

Dietrich Bonhoeffer

✠

'If only we had died by the hand of the LORD in the land of Egypt.'

Exodus 16.3

The people of Israel did not die on their way out of Egypt. Their long journey was a struggle that reformed and ultimately reconfigured them. They did not ever reach a land of milk and honey. Rather, it was their active engagement with their suffering which led them back to God. This new relationship with God helped them to see that the obsession with comfortable familiarity would disable them even more. A flight into ease would be a flight from themselves and a flight away from their deep and very real fears. Daring to ask, 'Who am I?' can be fruitful. Likewise, recognizing that we don't know who we are at times of instability opens up new possibilities. This is the time to place ourselves in God's hands and dare to say, 'I don't know who I am any more.' It may in fact be the safest and most fruitful place to be.

The Flight into Victory

'I will sing to the LORD, for he has triumphed gloriously; horse and rider he has thrown into the sea. The LORD is my strength and my might, and he has become my salvation.'

Exodus 15.1–2

A sudden illness will always get people talking. It ruptures the predictable ordinariness of life. Illness gives us something dramatic to talk about. It forces stories to be told, attracting listeners, co-writers and stage directors. Storytelling pits death against life with a protagonist who can be the hero, victim, warrior, soldier, princess or fool. Some of the story will be from our own memory, other parts may have been told to us, especially when we don't remember important scenes in the drama, or were absent from it through loss of consciousness or sleep. In an attempt to make sense of a traumatic and painful upheaval, like the people of Israel, we may long for a good battle too. Our situation can easily become a war of strength and will. Victory – a recovery from powerlessness and pain – may turn dangerously into a strutting macho stunt. Some with cancer find it offensive and tiring when people, often unthinkingly, use the term 'fighting cancer'. It sets them up for victory if the cancer is stopped, or defeat if the cancer results in death. An unfair burden is placed on sick shoulders like a yoke.

The Christian imperative is that death does not mean defeat, but rather, it makes way for us to be free with God.

In the book of Exodus the victory of escape through the Red Sea is remembered through song. This 'winning' overshadows their enslavement and testing journey. Triumph trumps everything; a swift and dramatic escape is the dominant chapter in this drawn-out story, propelling the people of Israel from slavery to freedom. Within this carefully constructed tale of recovery the existence of God is made reasonable when success is won, but God can be left behind once the fear has subsided and things seem safer and controllable.

Recovering from illness can be tedious. Minute improvements can occur in slow increments. Inconveniences – being unable to tie shoelaces or go to the toilet alone – demean us remorselessly. Our own personal assessments of recovery can be harsh and it is easy to blame ourselves for slow progress, as though our character is weak and our will is faint. No one wants to be called a wimp.

Our pain can be treated like an enemy within us that we imagine we can fight, 'if only we are strong enough'. But pain is our body crying out. Our pain is our own: we are the pain. We have to sit with it, but there is medication to help us on the way. I used to resist taking painkillers when the nurse came along the aisle of the ward with a rattling trolley like an ice-cream seller.

'Any pain? Want any painkillers, young lady?'

'Oh no, I'm fine. No thanks,' I said, grimacing through the ache in my forehead, my neck and my scalp.

I used to think that battling pain would win me medals, but I only gained premature wrinkles and became intoxicated by pride.

If we adopt a flight to victory in order to make quick sense of what illness is doing in us, or has done to us, we delude ourselves. There is no open goal soon reached when our bodies, memories, nerves and minds will effortlessly be at one again and everything will *soon be all right*, if not better than before our traumatic story began. We cannot rush recovery, but we can make informed choices in order to help our bodies recover. Mostly, we have to keep going. Plodding. Resting. Stumbling. Waiting.

I Am Who I Am

'"What is his name?" what shall I say to them?' God said to Moses, 'I AM WHO I AM.'

Exodus 3.13–14

Rather than a rush to a quick recovery, the journey requires a turning to one side. At the beginning of the book of Exodus when the possibility of a potential escape from slavery is rumbling, God reassures Moses that he will be there all the way. Such comfort is not reasonable to Moses who is terrified at the prospect of leadership. At an unexpected moment when he is shepherding his father-in-law's flock, a bush blazes. Something very strange is happening. Moses speaks to himself as though he has to convince himself, 'I must turn aside and look at this great sight, and see why the bush is not burned up' (Exodus 3.3).

The nature of God and his relationship with the people of Israel is revealed at this spectacular event: a bush is on fire but it is not being consumed by the flames. Moses stops and turns to see and here the nature and purpose of God is revealed:

'I am the God of your father, the God of Abraham, the God of Isaac, and the God of Jacob.'

Exodus 3.6

In the Hebrew language, in which this is originally written, the verb 'I am' is not at all static. Rather, God is revealed as one who is in a constant process of becoming. So God is full of potential, change and renewal. The 'I am' verb means much more, such as, 'I will be what I will be'. Moses' song of triumph would come 40 long years later. But he learned, in an ordinary day out alone with sheep which were not his possession, what his new identity would become. Crucially, it would be one of becoming rather than choosing. His identity would be created as he gathered and led God's people into a new place.

✠

R. S. Thomas's sonnet 'The Bright Field' captures the importance of noticing and stopping in order to make more sense of our identity and take stock of what is happening around us, and to us.

The Bright Field
I have seen the sun break through
to illuminate a small field
for a while, and gone my way
and forgotten it. But that was the
pearl of great price, the one field that had
treasure in it. I realize now
that I must give all that I have
to possess it. Life is not hurrying

on to a receding future, nor hankering after
an imagined past. It is the turning
aside like Moses to the miracle
of the lit bush, to a brightness
that seemed as transitory as your youth
once, but is the eternity that awaits you.

R. S. Thomas

If we are constantly running ahead both in our minds and our bodies, gifts and signs offered by God can easily go unseen, ignored or misunderstood.

We may notice something – 'the sun break through' – but not trust our intuition, or have the confidence or the tools to allow ourselves to be changed by a particular encounter or event. Being open to signs of spectacular ordinariness is something that those of us who are recovering from illness or a difficulty might do well to develop. An awareness of the potentiality of the everyday is important to us; the words used in the morning prayer liturgy reminds us of this:

> The night has passed, and the day lies open before us; let us pray with one heart and mind.
> As we rejoice in the gift of this new day, so may the light of your presence, O God, set our hearts on fire with love for you.

If prayer is tough at times, merely saying these few lines before lunch may make a difference.

Recovery can seem like endless drudgery if we are weighed down by pain or discomfort. Each day can be a tedious or even terrifying journey all of its own. Our eyes can become dull, half-closed by loss of confidence. Sometimes it can be easier not to see, not to look out for something that might be 'for us'.

Who are You?

> Jesus said to them, 'Very truly, I tell you, before Abraham was, I am.'
>
> John 8.58

Early in John's Gospel, he makes a direct connection to God's answer to Moses' enquiry of who is sending him. In Jesus is God enfleshed. God, who is being itself, enters the world and shares all that he is in his flesh. Later in this Gospel Jesus adds metaphors to his Father's abstract and even perhaps frustrating 'I AM'.

> 'I am the true vine'; 'I am the gate'; 'I am the good shepherd'. 'I am the light of the world.'
>
> John 15.1; 10.7; 10.11; 8.12

Before Jesus is arrested and crucified he prepares his disciples for the journey they will make once he is gone. Indeed, Jesus' arrest and crucifixion will cause them to make an exodus. They stumble, but they do survive, at least long enough to begin to make sense of God's purposes for the world in the person of their friend, Jesus.

'I have said these things to you to keep you from stumbling.'

John 16.1

After his arrest Jesus is handed over to be crucified and gives up his freedom. He makes his own journey beyond the city gates towards the crosses prepared for execution. Jesus makes an exodus in reverse. The Stations of the Cross placed around many church walls and pillars memorialize moments in Jesus' journey to his crucifixion. At the liturgy of the Stations of the Cross, we walk alongside him at stages which become increasingly gruesome and pitiful. God succumbs to passivity, humiliation and torture. At one station we pause to remember Jesus falling for the third time as his journey is halted again. He struggles along this Way to Golgotha, disabled now.

Almost annihilated and hanging on the cross, Jesus' last words are, 'I am thirsty.' Jesus, who in his life showed that he was a spring of new life from God the Father who created the world, is offered a sponge soaked in vinegar. It is a chilling moment completing Jesus' short life which started at the mother's breast.

Who am I?

For the cloud of the LORD was on the tabernacle by day, and fire was in the cloud by night, before the eyes of all the house of Israel at each stage of their journey.

Exodus 40.38

Here we have the final verse of the book of Exodus. Following the seemingly endless hardship it is eventually recognized that God has been with the Israelites all the way. The end of their journey is not a place at all. The end is a purpose, a *raison d'être*. The true purpose is in praise and prayer. Through worshipping God the people of Israel form their ultimate identity. Praise is the ground of their being, not a set of geographical coordinates.

✠

The neurologists proposed further surgery for me. I was sent to Sheffield Hallamshire Hospital where there was a brand-new machine designed to cauterize unstable blood vessels in the brain. It was the only such machine in Europe so I felt special. There was a long waiting list but the neurologist either pitied or liked me so there was no wait at all. I was given a room of my own looking westward towards the bleak but noble Pennines. Nurses were conspicuously attentive and I was soon suspicious. Flowers came too. The morning of my treatment I was given a tablet, to make me feel calm, they said. But after half an hour when they were moving me out of my room to receive the treatment I told them, 'It hasn't worked. I'm wide awake!'

I had taught myself to fight against anything trying to rule my body.

'You'll be OK,' said the nurse, smiling. They sat me up on the bed in a corridor. Someone got a razor out – a cheap plastic razor used to shave legs and chins.

'What are you doing?' I demanded.

I had an almost full head of long hair. It was growing back well, a year after its second shearing.

'Oh, don't worry; we have to make some space.'

'What space?'

Four patches were shaved, one at each side of my forehead and one at the left and right sides of the back of my head. And then a drill appeared. A DIY drill, just like the ones used to make holes in walls.

'What are you doing with that? What is that for?'

'Oh it's all right, Jennie, we just need to make room to put a frame on your head so that we know where to help your brain.'

'But . . .'

The bit of the drill broke through skin and bone.

A sweet-voiced nurse carried a square shaped metal contraption with rulers and screws on it.

'This needs to be put on safely so that you don't move your head in the machine. Your brain cells are precious aren't they, Jennie? It won't hurt, we promise. Deep breath for us now. Three more to go.'

I breathed shallow breaths. Again I fought against the faintness that was coming for me through black furry walls in my eyes. My dad says he can still smell my bones burning and see bone dust fizzing in the air.

'Well done Jennie. You're very brave. Only two more to go. Deep breath for us.'

The metal frame was clamped tight on my head in the four holes. I spent a whole day wearing it. Back then, many years before I would walk the way of the cross on Good Friday alongside others following Jesus' way to be crucified, I joked that it was like a crown of thorns. One of the nurses took a polaroid picture of me wearing that crown. I am pale, but I am beaming smiles for the camera.

I was moved along a conveyor belt towards a machine that looked like an igloo. I was locked into it by the head frame while nuclear gamma knives were beamed into my brain, evaporating any cells which might collapse and bleed. The doctor told me that it would take two years to see if the treatment had worked.

Before we crossed the Pennines home to Lancashire we went Christmas shopping in the shiny new retail park. I bought John a Teasmade machine for his bedside.

4

Faith

Strange things happen in the night – that phase when we seem least in control, where the boundaries of reality and fantasy are less rigid. We fear that danger may break in during the night, yet we often expect its entry too.

It was about six months after the treatment in Sheffield. The small shaved patches had lost ground and the holes on each temple side were closing up, leaving permanent white stains marking the day when I bore a metal crown. Again, my family and I presumed another clean break, and a fresh border was ours to build. We presumed that our time tramping between hospitals in the north-west was over. We thought that terrifying journey had ended.

I woke up from a deep sleep abruptly but there was no noise, no nightmares. I bolted upright but stayed in bed. My jaw started to jar to the left. These jagged mechanical movements were more powerful than twitching; there was a force and a violence to my chin switching quickly left to right about ten times, and the power was not mine. It stopped, I lay down, and went back to sleep.

'It's really weird. I woke up during the night and my mouth was kind of moving by itself', I mentioned to my mum just before she left for work.

'Hmm. Funny that, isn't it?'

It happened a second time but I didn't ask anyone to interpret it, neither did I connect it to my damaged brain. Despite the violence done to me by an invisible abnormality in my head, combined with people doing things to me, I did not like to admit it meant that it was less stable, and less *my own property* than before.

My body had become a mysterious stranger. For my parents my unpredictable body was completely terrifying.

Without consciously being aware of it my parents and I sacralized my body. It became a fragile, graced gift offered into the hands of doctors to be treasured and venerated by white-coated holy men serving in sanctuaries and neon-bright shrines. My parents cherished me: the whole me. But the concrete Jennie – my body – also contained the abstract Jennie – my spirit and my nature, which were held to ransom. Only the doctors who were guardians of my physical body could negotiate my whole release.

I was seized at school. It was an afternoon, during an English lesson – the only class I enjoyed, taught by Mrs Whiteside. There were chinks of humour beneath the heavily painted mask of hard-won authority. The desks were arranged in a horseshoe shape; mine was at the end of the line nearest the door at the very front of the classroom. We were reading *A Woman in White* by Wilkie Collins, a nineteenth-century detective story.

A silent rumbling ground through my gut, travelling fast, coming to get me, reaching like billowing fire to consume me from inside. My heart raced, terrified like an onlooker, a witness. The whoosh and the whirling thunder shuddered up my back and I sensed its force beginning to rage upwards towards my neck, my jaw, *my jaw*, my face. I bent forward from the waist, resting my forehead on the desk, unable to trust the more natural force of gravity. I began to move. Limbs jagged and sharp switched and my right arm winched itself above my head against my ear. My face became like hot blown glass nearing cooling point, resistant but certainly still pliable. That jaw, that chin slipped, stiff and bony to my left, and my full face followed it, trying to stay connected. I stood up, I should leave, I should escape. I fell forward to the floor on my knees, shaking, twitching, writhing. I heard a repetitive shrieking noise coming from the back of my throat, like a monkey warning its tribe that a predator was very close. Its rhythms matched the shake, the thud of me. Mrs Whiteside ran towards me but I fought, resisting her coercive touch. I was fighting my own body. Another English teacher, Mrs Halstead, came rushing in from the classroom next door and was shouting over my shrieks, 'Come on, Jennie, come on, it's all right. It's all right!'

But it was not all right at all. My body was all wrong.

I was unconscious, turning myself into an absent, monstrous, disastrous work of art for 30 other silenced pupils to interpret, just as they would the ridiculous Wilkie Collins novel without me.

I woke up as ambulance men carried me down the school stairs on a stretcher. I was driven to Blackburn Royal Infirmary where they gave me some pills to keep a raging force at bay. They diagnosed epilepsy but no one told me that I was epileptic. No one sat me down and said: you will have to change your life, this is not going to go away, you will be restricted, you will get hurt, this might kill you, you may cause offence, you will be injured, you will be judged, you will damage your brain each time it's let loose, drugs will harm and scar your body inside and out. No one said *I'm sorry.*

I took the drugs, phenytoin, without reading the list of side effects. I trusted them too much, just as I trusted doctors and my own body too much.

I was 16. I had completed my GCSE exams, left school and was living with a family in Paris on a year abroad programme. I decided that, as the government could no longer dictate how I used the limited time I had left to live, I needed to push on quick and adventure. I was convinced I would be dead before I reached 21. I wanted to leave Baxenden, to travel abroad, speak a foreign language fluently, create my own adventures rather than allow my body to trick me and trip me up. I decided that I owned my body; I knew but could not accept that it was not mine to possess. I had to learn ways to be possessed and allow possession.

It was warm in the northern Paris suburb and I was sitting on the doorstep listening to a cassette playing music, reading a letter from John who was studying in London. No one else was at home. Delicate pins and needles sprinkled my nose so I scratched it. I felt ants crawling underneath the skin on my cheeks, my forehead and lips. I went inside the house, closing the door. The itchy sensation had evaporated; now a roar inside me was grinding up speed towards my chest, feeding on the air in my lungs. A steady wave pulsed up my neck. I ran into the hallway; there was a phone on a shelf there. My arms began to twitch and the wave was hollowing out my mouth, but my mouth and my arms would not fall away yet. I battered out my home phone number in Lancashire.

'Hello?' my dad answered. It was early afternoon and he was home from his 5 a.m. shift.

My hand shook and jostled with the receiver. 'It's me.' It jumped out of my hand; my knees crumpled, my head jerked, my lips melted but I voiced my cry before I was taken hostage. *'I'm having a fit.'*

'Jennie! Jennie!' he shouted. 'OK? All right! Jennie? Jennie?'

Hearing a gruff snore woke me. The B52s cassette was still playing. It was on auto repeat so I have no idea how long I was fitting, unconscious or sleeping. I did not move but remained on the stone floor in the hall. I heard male voices, they were close, very close. They were wearing navy clothes and speaking loudly in French. I remember nothing more.

After I dropped the phone my dad ran outside, hoping that someone would be able to help him decide what to do but there was no one. He phoned the school where my mum worked. He asked if the head teacher, Ron, would help. Ron found a number for international rescue whose headquarters were in Glasgow and told the person at the switchboard my address in France. In less than an hour a rescue squad broke through the door in Paris. My dad later told me that he had a terrifying split decision to make – should he keep me on the phone, or hang up and phone someone for help?

'I've never been the same since,' he said. Soon after he developed severe panic attacks which held him hostage too.

My scarred brain's faulty energy began to creep up on me during the night again and again, incongruously but begrudgingly familiar. Many of them seem to happen during the night. Each time I have a seizure a tickling fuzziness draws me out of sleep like a radio alarm that starts out gently then rises to an unignorable volume. A rumbling swish rises from the pit of my gut and my heart throbs loud and fast, aware it has a sprint on.

Every time this happens Amy, my partner, wakes up, shoots up with the arrow speed and intent of one who has heard an intruder enter. She has become finely attuned to subtle whims and whiffs of the auras that breathe into my body, charging the bed invisibly. Our bed becomes a stage. We have developed lines and roles, places and movements to let the derangement act itself out. My body, not myself, is the villain, the genie, the devil.

'I'm having a fit,' I say, confessing the terrible truth to myself as much as to her. I kneel on the bed like a stunned but well-trained dog.

'It's OK. I'm here. I'm here with you.' And we wait for the force to gather pace and find weak spots in my brain. This preparation is like a death-bed experience. I sometimes wonder whether, when that time does come for me to die, the feeling will be familiar.

Only the bedside lamp is lit. The main light would reveal too many gruesome contortions. The covers are swept away: blankets and pillows are lethal because they can suffocate. Separately and jointly we prepare ourselves for the brute force to embed itself and reach every cell, ligament and bone in a raging and rampant swoop.

'It's all right sweetie. I'm here.' She kneels in bed above me, leaving space but staying close. The bed becomes her battlefield as much as it is mine.

'Rub my back.'

'Here we go. I'm rubbing your back. You'll be safe. I'm with you. I'm here with you. I'm here.'

'Sing with me.'

Adoramus te domino, quoniam bonus . . .

Amy joins in the Latin Taizé prayer chant with me. It is sung in a half superstitious, half-wretched attempt to sing in *Latin* to create a foreign decoy. Anything to prevent the electric charge from travelling further through my brain and rampaging through my body. We scratch and rub my thumbs like frenzied crack addicts soon to score, hoping to find another way to interrupt the electrical pathway through my brain. If it finds a way forward, my body and consciousness will not be mine for a while.

'I'm with you here Jennie. OK, we'll be all right.'

It is easy to fall, hit myself or suffocate. There are so many ways to die during a seizure. One in every 1,000 people die from Sudden Unexplained Death from Epilepsy (SUDEP). That's 1,200 people every year. Three people die having an epileptic fit in Britain every day. The heart runs out of steam, breathing stops, the body is clamped shut: *seized*. Sometimes it just kills you.

Amy clears away any dangers as a mother would a playpen, but she is not my mother, she is the love of my life. She cannot control, she can only attempt to mitigate damage. With the stage set, Amy can only be a spectator now.

And then my jaw hardens and twitches to the left at a steady pace like a broken robot. My right shoulder socket begins to grind and a raging force stampedes along my arms and fingers, turning them rigid as stone. Sometimes my right arm lifts, pulled up as if a string is attached to my wrist. But it is the electric charge, starting at the scarred cerebral zone and triggered by fatigue or stress which en-fleshes and en-bones itself in me.

I often wet the bed. The physical spasms reach organs as well as limbs. Amy has to decide whether to wake me out of unconsciousness to pat me dry, or to wait for my body to wake itself. The medical term for this awakening is 'postictal'. It is a Latin term which means 'after a blow'. Most of the time I wake up in words. Eyes closed, I am told that I speak a language of tongues: a post-seizure gobbledegook. These utterances, with their own grammar and syntax are not for an audience, they are the residue of deranged electrical activity.

Dawn. Sheets changed, my body cleaned, dried and smoothed out calm, Amy waits and watches. She cannot leave the house. She checks and checks again: still breathing, unbroken. When I open my eyes she is close to my face, smiling with compassion like Christ's.

Exile

Arise, cry out in the night,
    at the beginning of the watches!
Pour out your heart like water
    before the presence of the Lord!

Lamentations 2.19

The land of milk and honey God promised to the people of Israel as they left Egypt was not a real place anyway. They did reach their destination – the land of Canaan – but they did not stop there for long. Their identity and their faith was not completed and sealed on entering Canaan. In the sixth century BC when the Babylonians bombarded Jerusalem, the city was sacked and the Temple was destroyed. Almost the entire population was sent into exile. New and hitherto unimaginable forms of discomfort, torment and loss were discovered. Everything was strange: foreignness was everywhere, even within themselves, both personally and collectively. Their faith was tested, stretched, yet ultimately transformed by this shocking upheaval.

✠

Most people take their bodies for granted, at least when they are young. When illness or accident strikes we can soon discover that our flesh, blood and bones feel separate from us and believe that our body is working – even conspiring – against us. The unspoken trust which normally flows between our selves and our bodies can break down quickly. When faith in our body's neat and discrete ways crumbles, we can feel like strangers in the land of our own bodies.

From an early age our bodies flourish as well-kept concerns: watered, fed, cherished and appreciated. As our bodies change and grow, some become stunningly beautiful, some large and powerful, others weaker, but each one is unique. Some are obsessed with bodily upkeep, others are ashamed of their bodies and neglectful. When all is well with our bodies we can feel safe and at one with ourselves and our environment. Yet we can delude ourselves that our bodies are owned, secure and self-sufficient.

When we are in pain and our bodies are in distress we are forced to let our defences down. Incisions, scans, endoscopies, smears, can feel like violations. Turned over by unrecognizable gloved hands, wearing a laundered and recycled backless gown, we can feel assaulted as we are tested with sharp pricks, shots, tubes and electrical jolts. Have our bodies been taken hostage? Somehow, suddenly, others own it. Bleeding, seeping, sagging flesh hangs like meat. Lolling tongues, whoops of pain, incontinence: our bodies, estranged from our memories and our mirrors, are an undignified denigration of our once so proud, once so potent, glorious body. Even those who have helped and appreciate us can seem to be part of this militia invading our suddenly defenceless bodies and are unable to interpret the new languages our bodies are speaking. As we lie in terror our bodies are occupied by forces of pain in, on and around us, beyond the walls of our own skin. The glorious city of our body is sacked. We are strange bodies in strange lands.

Lamentation

How lonely sits the city
  that once was full of people!
How like a widow she has become,
  she that was great among the nations!
She that was a princess among the provinces
  has become a vassal.

Lamentations 1.1

The book of Lamentations is a small, easily missable book of the Old Testament. In the Church's lectionary a short verse is normally extracted from the neatly ordered set of five poems in the last three days of Holy Week. Disorientation, loathing, desolation, anger, fear and raw emotion are expressed here. Following the tale of the death of loved ones, loss of land and property, we learn that the poet's entire existence has been torn apart. This loss is grounded, however, in the city of Jerusalem: God's glorious dwelling place. God's promise of peace, God's presence and fullness of life, has been broken down through the pillaging by a greedy and remorseless power.

'Is this the city that was called the perfection of beauty, the joy of all the earth?'

Lamentations 2.15

In Lamentations we read that a unique covenant is abandoned and we hear the voice of one individual, on behalf of the people of Israel, trying to understand what has happened. Personal pain and collective identity come together here: the city is destroyed, the people are in physical and emotional pain and everyone is forced to survive in a foreign land. Ultimately, God is believed to have abandoned them. Tragedy strikes everywhere. Faith in God has become a traumatic idea in itself.

We find five poems, probably written by one person. The Lament genre – *qina* – which means 'Oh why?' is used to give voice and form to the chaotic despair that the shock of homelessness, damage and dislocation has created by exile. The metre is fixed, lines are neat and repetitions are memorable. Each poem creates an acrostic (the first letter of each line of Lamentations spells out the 22 letters of the Hebrew alphabet). The acrostic form was perhaps a learning tool and an aid to help others memorize the poetry. The one thing that can be manipulated in this time of absence and distress is language. There is no need to explain the situation because all those using it are in it. As meaning has broken down, words and form are grappled with in order to construct order among chaos. The struggle to create a modicum of order does not fix much, but it may help to sift through experience, memory and tradition. No one can take these treasures away.

Three themes are expressed in this series of poems: shame, confession and hope. First, the poet reflects on the past: being led from Egypt, the creation of a covenant, the inheritance of land, and Israel's disobedience. Next, the poet explores the present situation, speaking to God in confession. Each line is an act of faith. God is not absent, but is sometimes viewed as a despotic destroyer. Finally the poet looks to the future, pleads for God to return, forgive and save.

✠

In times of deep anxiety, when loss and powerlessness invade, these themes create for us a template for the crisis of faith. Poetic form, with its traditional rules and respect for language and structure, provides the writer and reader with an honourable frame to cling to. I find poetry to be a rich resource. When I am afraid poetry sometimes gives words, structure and form to my anxiety or despair.

Paula Meehan's poem offers an example of how the gently restraining forces of form allow deep sorrow to be expressed and honoured. Creating poetry becomes an act of faith in itself when something or someone is lost.

Child Burial
Your coffin looked unreal,
fancy as a wedding cake.

I chose your grave clothes with care,
your favourite stripy shirt,

your blue cotton trousers.
They smelt of woodsmoke, of October,

your own smell there too.
I chose a gansy of handspun wool,

warm and fleecy for you. It is
So cold down in the dark.

No light can reach you and teach you
the paths of wild birds,

The name of flowers,
The fishes, the creatures.

Ignorant you must remain
of the sun and its work,

my lamb, my calf, my eaglet,
my cub, my kid, my nestling,

my suckling, my colt. I would spin
time back, take you again

within my womb, your amniotic lair,
and further spin you back

through nine waxing months
to the split seeding moment

you chose to be made flesh,
word within me.

I'd cancel the love feast
the hot night of your making.

I would travel alone
to a quiet mossy place,

You would spill from me into the earth
Drop by bright red drop.

Paula Meehan

Some poetry that is created by despair has the paradoxical ability to create 'sword-set beauty', a stunning image found in Rowan Williams' poem 'Advent Calendar'. Moreover, Williams offers us an astonishing example of restraint in the face of desperation, and hopeful anticipation in spite of the terrible reality of emptiness. Faith in God is not to be taken for granted. Rather, it is the unceasing activity of obedient curiosity in what might happen, in what could be. Jesus Christ embodies God's desire to bring relief and comfort. The gift of Jesus Christ in the world reassures us that we can cry out to God in order to feel found and be known.

Advent Calendar
He will come like last leaf's fall.
One night when the November wind
has flayed the trees to bone, and earth
wakes choking on the mould,
the soft shroud's folding.

He will come like frost.
One morning when the shrinking earth
opens on mist, to find itself
arrested in the net
of alien, sword-set beauty.

He will come like dark.
One evening when the bursting red
December sun draws up the sheet

and penny-masks its eye to yield
the star-snowed fields of sky.

He will come, will come,
will come like crying in the night,
like blood, like breaking,
as the earth writhes to toss him free.
He will come like child.

Rowan Williams

Lord save me!

When the disciples saw him walking on the lake, they were terrified, saying 'It is a ghost!' And they cried out in fear. But immediately Jesus spoke to them and said, 'Take heart, it is I; do not be afraid.'

Peter answered him, 'Lord, if it is you, command me to come to you on the water.' He said, 'Come.' So Peter got out of the boat, started walking on the water, and came towards Jesus. But when he noticed the strong wind, he became frightened, and beginning to sink, he cried out, 'Lord, save me!' Jesus immediately reached out his hand and caught him, saying to him, 'You of little faith, why did you doubt?'

Matthew 14.26–32

Most of us have cried out to God for help when we have been in a dire situation; it is as natural as sneezing. But what do we expect of God when we do cry out, 'Lord, save me?' In Matthew's Gospel Peter does just that. The disciples are in trouble on the lake. Unbidden, Christ comes towards them but they don't recognize him. Jesus' wish to be with them in trouble is not understood and it will not be until he returns, resurrected. On the lake Jesus is 'Here I am' once again as he says to the disciples in the unstable boat, 'Take heart, it is I.' We see an intimate encounter between Peter and Jesus. Peter is compelled to draw nearer to him, beyond the ordinary: 'let me be where you are,' he thinks. And Jesus draws him closer indeed. Peter welcomes the encouragement but soon he loses sight, imagination and trust in who Jesus is. Nevertheless, when he begins to lose faith in that exquisite moment Peter cries out for help, and like a mother, Jesus protects him. He knows.

> How could we sing the LORD's song
>   in a foreign land?
> If I forget you, O Jerusalem,
>   let my right hand wither!
>
> Psalm 137.4–5

Crying out for help runs through the book of Psalms. For those who pray regularly with the psalms it is something we try to live out as we pray with them. The psalms are our tools: people have been in trouble before and written these verses, chanted them, sung and pondered them. So many of the psalms arose out of distress. The psalms are precious gifts and there are 150 in the Bible offered to find homes under our skin, under our breath. Sometimes the psalms give us words to use in order to ask God to remember us. Yet God does not need to be told to remember us. Rather, in our inheritance of the psalms we can remind ourselves that we would do well to try to cling and keep clinging on to God. Even when we might feel estranged from the psalmist's words they are there to make home in our bodies, finding places in gaps of fear and anguish, echoing, crying out, worshipping, praising for us, in us and with us. Our bodies, like Mary, can become God-bearers if we keep faith like this.

Finding Rest

> Answer me when I call, O God of my right!
>   You gave me room when I was in distress.
>   Be gracious to me, and hear my prayer
>
> Psalm 4.1

Compline, also known as Night Prayer, is one of the most beautiful services in the Church's liturgy. Its title comes from the Latin word *completio*, meaning completion. It is a form of words, poetry and prayers which help us to complete our day well. Perhaps more profoundly, Compline allows us to 'complete' our lives in preparation for death and in the hope of the resurrection where light will shine and a new day and a new creation will begin. Compline is short, quiet and easy to memorize. The service begins in the dark, in the west where the sun has set. The liturgy is simultaneously a reflection on the day about to close and on a life about to end. Silent reflection on the day and confession of the things that are on our conscience mirrors the ministry of anointing which a priest gives to the sick and dying. A song of thanks follows for all that God is and has done for us in the day – and indeed our life. And then the psalms follow. When they are quietly chanted in dimly lit chapels and monasteries it can be very moving. Fragments from Psalm 17 follow the short Bible reading:

> Keep me as the apple of your eye; hide me under the shadow of your wings.
>
> Psalm 17.8

These words help us to acknowledge that we are afraid. We are not the first people to ask for help from the One we cannot see. We can only believe. We are given the words children ask, or wish they could ask, of their parents: Are you there? Am I safe? Do you love me? Am I special?

Towards the end of Compline we sing Simeon's canticle from Luke's Gospel:

> Now, Lord, you let your servant go in peace,
> your word has been fulfilled.
> My own eyes have seen the salvation
> which you have prepared in the sight of every people;
> A light to reveal you to the nations
> and the glory of your people Israel.
>
> Luke 2.29–32

When we sing or say these words we become that ancient faithful man who waited for the arrival of the longed-for Messiah and we can make his poetry our own in the Compline liturgy: *'Have*

I seen Christ today?' Yes? So I can sleep – it will be all right. Likewise, looking back at my life in preparation for death and the expectation of a new life: *'Have I ever witnessed and taken hold of Christ in one way or another?'* Yes? I can die now. I am set free.

Finally, in the service we remind ourselves that darkness and death does not reign. We must look eastward. The new light that we will see in the morning and in heaven too will be brought in by the risen Christ. As we live in our changed bodies we can have faith that Christ will appear and make himself known. These are the closing lines of the service of Compline:

As the night watch looks for the morning
so do we look for you, O Christ.

✠

I have had many MRI (magnetic resonance imaging) scans on my brain over the years. Cumbersome MRI machines show abnormalities in fine detail that would otherwise be impossible to pick up with other non-invasive treatment. It is much safer than opening up the skull or injecting dye. For an MRI brain scan I lie on my back with my head couched in a frame to keep it absolutely still. Then I am moved on a conveyer belt into the middle of the machine, which looks like an enormous plastic egg box. My face is inches from the inside wall of the machine. It is claustrophobic, and for some it must feel like being buried alive. The noise is terrible: loud and screeching. Some hospitals offer music to listen through headphones to cover up the noise. Although the intention is generous the music is deafened by the banging magnets. As the magnets collide my body moves. Twitching limbs terrifies me even more as I have to decide what twitches are magnetic and external, and which are electrical and internal. The radiographers are able to speak to the patient via a microphone and do so tenderly because they are fully aware that, even though an MRI scan is not painful, it is not an easy or comfortable experience. There is a panic button to press in case the patient feels distressed. I have never had the courage to press the panic button although every

time I have felt desperate to escape. Whenever I have an MRI scan
I recite Compline: three times, sometimes more. It is my treasure.

> Whoever dwells in the shelter of the Most High
> and abides under the shadow of the Almighty,
> Shall say to the Lord, 'My refuge and my stronghold,
> my God in whom I put my trust.'
>
> Psalm 91.1–2, sung at Compline.

Faith in Foreign Land

On a quest to recovery we could think of faith as a journey into
transformation. Post-illness 'home' may never be the same again.
Disfigured, scarred, weary, bored, afraid, we attempt to move forward to some measure of comfort. We cannot walk back, only
away from the fear and terror we felt when illness struck.

When life is good and death does not seem real or close by it is
easy to presume that faith is something done for us. We learned
about God at school and then shelved him away next to the multi-
plication tables. Just as we may have taken our bodies for granted
when our health was robust, so may we have taken the gift of
faith for granted too. It is easy to convert faith into memory in
fair weather. We must make faith real ourselves and we can make
our bodies a home for faith, a dwelling place for God as we travel
to recover God and recover ourselves. Faith is a gift offered as a
way of life.

If faith is primarily founded on grand concepts of God as
Father, Lord, Almighty, King of the universe, glorious in majesty,
then God's presence among the endless minutiae of a sick body's
needs may not easily convince us that God will come anywhere
near. Instead, we can rail against God, actively refusing to make
God part of our healing process. Our prolonged experience of
pain may function as paradoxically energizing proof that God
does not exist. Worse than this though, is to develop a more damaging kind of belief: I must have done something wrong to deserve
all this.

The book of Job is a masterful work of poetry. It tests that question: Why does God let bad things happen to good people? Alongside God and the devil the reader becomes the audience as Job demands advice from his friends. The calamities which fall on Job could not be more extreme: his family perish, he has no job, no money, no home. We watch Job shake his fist to heaven as he desperately tries to understand what has happened to him, and why. Like the psalmists he gives us words of despair and cries of injustice that echo our own:

'I loathe my life;
 I will give free utterance to my complaint;
 I will speak in the bitterness of my soul,
I will say to God, Do not condemn me;
 let me know why you contend against me.'

Job 10.1-2

Job is desperate to understand his feelings of suffering. But he can find no meaning in his experience; everything seems absurd: there is no logic to it. His view of God does not fit neatly into his personal crisis. He searches for any wrongdoing in his life but is unable to balance his petty misdemeanours with the depth of his sufferings. His friends offer anodyne platitudes. For these men who seem never to have suffered, God is entirely reasonable. They are keen for Job to recover quickly, to be quiet and return to his entirely comprehensible faith. It is in Job's lyrical crying out and his tireless questioning of the previously unquestionable that his complete estrangement is made even more real – and terrifying. Job refuses to turn away from God but also refuses to keep silent. The final paragraph of chapter 31 consists of only six words:

The words of Job are ended.

Job 31.40

His fugue of questions and challenges is complete; his storm has blown itself out. But the puzzle of suffering is not solved; this is not the end of the drama. Job never entirely runs out of hope and words. Entirely unexpectedly, God reveals himself in a whirlwind:

'Gird up your loins like a man,
I will question you, and you shall declare to me.'

Job 38.3

God urges Job to look around him to recognize the full active
reality of God. Job is required to look beyond himself – to forget
himself for a while, to allow awe into his vision. God's response is
kaleidoscopic – his revelation uncovers more and more evidence of
his nature and identity. Job watches, listens, dreams, remembers,
imagines and lays his hand on his mouth, silenced and stunned by
it all. And then comes his response:

Then Job answered the LORD:
'I know that you can do all things,
    and that no purpose of yours can be thwarted.
"Who is this that hides counsel without knowledge?"
Therefore I have uttered what I did not understand,
    things too wonderful for me, which I did not know.
"Hear, and I will speak;
    I will question you, and you declare to me."
I had heard of you by the hearing of the ear,
    but now my eye sees you;
therefore I despise myself,
    and repent in dust and ashes.'

Job 42.1–6

Job's resilience and imagination allow him to recognize God and
be humbled by God's glory. He did not turn away from God. Yet
although he could not understand faith's purpose, his sense that
God exists could not be eradicated. Ultimately, Job lived faithfully, neither knowing nor understanding why he suffered. The
story ends with Job being restored to his kith and kin, a completely changed man.

Job learns to enlarge his vision of his faith in God; he is free to
expect more from God. In our narrow view of God we may find
no room for him in the new physical and psychological landscape

that illness creates. God can become easier to live without because he just doesn't fit so neatly. We suspect that God demands too much from us; perhaps we feel that we just don't have the energy to muster our best behaviour.

Being Found

We must remember that faith in God is an invitation, not a command. Exiled from work, home, friends and status, illness can make faith seem naive. Faith is a force of life which God desires to share with us. Our breath, our heartbeats are sourced by God and are inseparable from God. Our exiled bodies are places where God can make a dwelling. When we are most estranged, God is most at home. Prayers and words, Scripture and poetry may feel like a foreign language when we are recovering. Such richness and complexity may feel like an affront to our tedious recovery, but they are there for us to hold on to, to ingest, digest and make our own.

The writer of Lamentations had to find her own words in order to hold on to her past, to keep going in the present and to conceptualize a future. The writer created a home for God within the lines of poetry that were later copied, memorized and continue to be recited today.

We can house these words as structures, foundations of our faith when we have no words of our own to match up to the strange world our sick bodies have been pushed into.

> He shot into my vitals
>   the arrows of his quiver;
> I have become the laughing-stock of all my people,
>   the object of their taunt-songs all day long.
> He has filled me with bitterness,
>   he has glutted me with wormwood.
>
> Lamentations 3.13–15

Christ's experience of desolation was not something expected; no one but Jesus himself could conceive it. Only a few women and one beloved disciple stayed to watch him suffer and expire on the cross. God made himself at home in the world and, keeping faith with God the Father, Jesus became an exile.

Why, O LORD, do you stand far off?
Why do you hide yourself in times of trouble?

Psalm 10.1

5

Vocation

On Sundays, when I was about ten, my dad used to take me to an empty supermarket car park to teach me how to drive. He explained how the three pedals worked, familiarized me with the four coordinates of the gear stick and put me in the driver's seat. Tall for my age, but still peering over the wheel, I was multitasking before I knew the phrase even existed. Left or right, *I* was deciding which way to turn; soon we were moving faster than I walked to school. As we travelled, my dad hands-free, I felt grown-up and well on my way to freedom.

A year later in the outpatients wing of the Pendlebury Children's Hospital my dad and I were called into Mr R. A. C. Jones' consulting room for a routine check-up. He sat behind an enormous desk. His grandiosity was half-performed, half-honed by the privileges of education and hard-earned respect. As we watched, the performer, shifting by instinct, loomed forward and spoke like a public school headmaster consigned to a spell in a reception class on a council estate.

'Well, well well, how well *we* look Miss Hogan! *So* fit and healthy!'

I had said nothing, though I *had* walked in and sat down unaided, grinning as good girls must. He shifted his eyes towards my father, 'Isn't she looking good, Dad?'

My father reddened and nodded, silenced by a man who sounded like one of the school teachers who threw blackboard brushes his way. I blushed too, half wanting the charade to be over, half desperate to know what was going to happen to me. Was I healthy? When would I die? Was it all over because the doctor pronounced me fixed by looking into my eyes and seeing my flushed face? Would I never see him again?

Then he leaned towards us, Shakespearian in his hushed aside, 'I have to tell you one thing though.' His brow furrowed, his show had become a pantomime. 'You won't ever be able to drive, Jennie.'

I pulled back into the plastic seat and bit my lower lip as I dropped my chin.

'But fabulous to see you! Jolly good. That's it now – off you go! Thanks, Dad!'

We backed our way out, bowing at the act before our quick exit.

I hardly noticed that I lost a left-sided portion of my vision following the first bleed. Did I not *see it*? My partial loss of sight was not explained to me, or at least not confirmed to me, so – strangely – I did not *see* what I could not see.

At primary school I remained captain of the netball team. My position was 'Centre', which meant that I could attack and defend on most of the court. My sight loss was not an impediment. To impede: to prevent, or obstruct; from the Latin *impedire*, to shackle the feet, to stop the foot. I could not drive, but I could still race.

At Hollins School I became captain of the netball and hockey teams. Miss Cooper, our PE teacher, even asked me to play in the teams for the year above. We didn't win much, but no one bashed my teeth out with a hockey stick; I must have been able to see one coming because quite a few came close. Youth, vigour and doggedness may have closed my eyes to what I could not do. In those *entre deux guerres* years between the first and second brain haemorrhage, being alive was synonymous with *yes!*

Aged 14, the second haemorrhage struck. I lay in a bed in the high dependency ward in Hope Hospital, Salford. Following the emergency surgery, I thawed into an awareness of being, sensing existence that was still mine. I was sore and conscious. There was a ceiling. It looked small, squashed. Caving in? No: *just wrong*. Alive, awake, I sensed and soon admitted to myself that I was somehow partially imprisoned in my body. I remembered that fuzzy muzzledness from before and the physical sense of entrapment was more of a 'not yet' than a 'no'. It would pass. But opening my eyes, watching the brightly lit ceiling I felt suffocated though I could breathe easily. What I saw was more like a dark malevolent presence in my sight that was not lifting with each blink.

Half of the world had disappeared. Exactly half, symmetrically, straight down the middle in each eye. I was given an eye patch to wear but no one explained why because there was no open wound on my eye and the pupils and the whites of my eyes were unchanged: nothing looked different from the outside. Nothing on the surface of my eyes revealed the new emptiness I saw. Although the plastic patch further collapsed every object before me it provided an outward sign of an inward fault. People still fail to believe me when I explain what I see or do not see; their eyes glaze over, it is not interesting, not sexy because there is nothing to gawp at. My blindness can only be seen on scans and screens or by my actions. A clumsy person is inarguably lazy, irresponsible – childish – unworthy of assistance. Silly woman. She should look where she's going.

When a bleed in the brain occurs it can interrupt optic nerves and pathways. Three in five haemorrhagic strokes, like the one I had, change a person's vision in some way or another. This can range widely, from difficulty in moving eyes, blurred vision, even to complete sight loss. Some people are lucky and find that their sight loss improves, or even disappears as the brain recovers. Perhaps that happened to me following my first bleed. How could I have played team sports so well with a collapsed world? No further testing was done, so perhaps it did improve for just a few years. Perhaps Mr Jones, working in the operating theatre, saw something in the raw material of my brain with his own eyes that I could not with mine.

There is a term for my visual deficit: *homonomous hemianopia*. It is Greek which means, 'inability to see half on one side'. It names perfectly, if abstractly, what the bleed in my brain did to my sight. An additional description was only recently given to my sight loss following a neuropsychological psychometric test. The *homonomous hemianopia* is 'dense'. Yes – the deficit is thick, muddy and stubborn. Yet I suppose there is a musicality in its beautifully geometric patterning and reveals how each left and right hemisphere of our brains collaborate or war with each other.

At the time of the second haemorrhage I was given multiple visual field confrontation tests. I had to stare at the doctor's nose while he (it always was a he) would move and twitch his fingers asking me to say when I saw them. The range of peripheral vision on my right side is completely normal, so testing stopped on that side. The doctor raised his fingers in front of me at my left side, and even very close to his nose I could not see, never mind *count his fingers*. Other times he would move his fingers from my far-left side with an outstretched arm, moving gradually towards his nose and the central point of my vision. Each time I would only see his fingertips when it reached his right nostril. His nose twitched and his eyes widened, amazed and confused every time when I said, 'Now I see it!' What a spectacle. But the doctor did not name it, or explain it. No one told me what effect this may have on my life. I already knew I could not drive. Was that it?

Tests more nuanced than finger wagging exist now. A Goldmann perimetry machine is shaped like half a hollowed-out egg on its side with a chinrest at the base. One eye is covered and a buzzer is put in the patient's hand. Each time I see a light appear like a star burst, sometimes bright, sometimes small and faint, I have to press the buzzer. The machine translates this into an eye-shaped black and white image of what I can and cannot see. When I saw my Goldmann report for the first time in 2007 it was like being shown a human skeleton, where something that I know is there but cannot fully see myself was revealed. An image of my sight was reflected back to me and my understanding of, and relationship with my body immediately deepened and expanded. Two pieces of paper, one for each eye, became flags vindicating what I suspected my bleeding brain had created. The ophthalmologist at Moorfields Eye Hospital was astonished that I was not registered as partially sighted. A Certificate of Visual Impairment (CVI) was issued immediately. It became prized and incontestable proof of the irreversible damage done.

There is no surgical treatment to recover a person's sight following damage to the brain. The neural systems between the brain and the eyes are sophisticated; what is gone is gone. There are neurological rehabilitation programmes available now; strategies can be learned to fend off the emptiness by training the brain to expect to see more, to look harder and wider. There are also methods and tools available to encourage a person to use eye movements creatively. Mirrored prisms placed in spectacles to widen the visual field exist too. It is curious that I have never been offered such resources and I am sorry that I didn't know about them until recently. When I move my eyes to the left of my visual field in order to see more it is like entering into unfamiliar territory; it is uncomfortable going into the absent vision. My eyes hurt and I worry people might see and treat me as a blind person with funny rolling eyes.

I did not easily adopt smart ways to compensate for the loss of half of my visual field, such as sitting in a particular place in a room, or checking to see who might be silently lurking to my left. I did not adapt my neck to sit comfortably and subtly askew, making room for my face to turn obliquely to the left at each face before me. I did not hold books at a sharper angle; I did not check or gauge whether my reading speed had slowed. It was only when I began to read aloud in church that I realized how difficult the printed word is for me to see. I often lose my place; it takes time to find the beginning of a line; I guess words. For example, the word may be 'mouth', but I miss the first letter and guess 'south'. I take much longer than a fully sighted person to scan a scene: birdwatching is useless, although I do have a pair of binoculars. I trip up daily, ruin shoes, bump into people and discover bruises everywhere on my body from forgettable falls. I see half a screen in the cinema, half a face before me, and half a page. I burn myself when cooking, smash plates, bang into walls, bikes, bollards. I ignore acquaintances walking down the street, groups at parties, waiters in restaurants. I must have dismissed thousands of handshakes – unseeing the person's right hand stretched out expectantly towards me on my left; ignorant of the polite gesture, I suppose I must smile innocently while their hand is retracted when I fail to reciprocate.

I believe in miracles: a bus has not yet flattened me.

I now see that youth, vigour and doggedness must have closed my eyes to what I could not do. I kept my blindness as a secret, knowingly and unknowingly absorbing the shame that my limitations endlessly invited. I would not insist that I walk at a person's right in a liturgical procession so I could keep in alignment; I would not make sure that I found the right seat in a lecture hall, or in a pew that did not exclude every other person from my field of sight. Blindness is lonely and if it is not lived well it invites endless waves of embarrassment and can erode dignity, freedom and identity.

Blindness imposes itself on me and in me. My not seeing half suffocates and hinders me the moment I open my eyes. A whole half hems me in; not quite a blackness to be challenged, more like an unpredictable vacuum sucking half the world out of my experience of being alive. While my sight loss is perfectly balanced, my navigation of the world is not. My dreams, however, are prolific and panoramic: I wonder – what do we see and how do we see in heaven?

When I was given the Certificate of Visual Impairment a copy of it was automatically sent to my local authority. As a result, I was visited by the disability team in Tower Hamlets Council, where we were living at the time, led by a blind social worker. Did I want a guide dog? an emergency alarm? a counsellor? a white stick? I said yes to each offering, except the dog.

I have a white symbol cane. It is slim, about a centimetre thick, half a metre long and folds into three, with a thin elastic wristband at one end. It is light and fits unobtrusively into a small bag. Ironically the symbolism of the cane adds so much *blindness* to my already multifaceted outward identity – a redhead with a neat quiff, masculine presenting person, priest . . . I noticed that people only saw my blindness; they assumed that I could not see anything. The only thing they could see was that I was blind. Any white stick of any size in public seems to signify total blindness, regardless of my discrete symbol cane. Yet without my symbol cane I find that supermarkets, shopping centres and train stations are the most problematic zones. People rush in from all directions and I easily become disorientated, bumped, insulted, shocked and startled as bodies jump into my central vision, often causing physically painful and embarrassing collisions. Many people instantly assume that I am rude, bullish or careless. Sometimes I explain, pitifully, that I am partially sighted. I have been hit, spat at, and I am often verbally abused or tutted at. When I dare carry the symbol cane I feel like Moses at the parting of the Red Sea because people generously make a safe way for me to walk. But they see the stick first, then my lack, then the fool, and finally, the person. I am in the blind closet, gradually coming out.

Immediately following my second bleed the perfectly symmetrical left-sided paralysis of my body was obvious. I could not hold a pen or a fork. I could not walk or circle my foot. My hand was still like a claw. Visitors stared at my limbs, willing them to become supple. My youth, committed focus, and intensive rehabilitation rewired and soldered some of the cut-off networks that the bleed in my brain had severed. Walking, eating and waving unaided marked the goal of complete recovery. But the invisible blockages that dammed my range of vision many years ago were never eased open and still remain shut.

We had a party to celebrate my mother's fortieth birthday in the summer, just a few months after my return from my second stay in hospital. My dad presided over the barbecue in our back garden. As I hobbled towards him I lost my balance and toppled on to the barbecue heavily, as though my left side was weighted on a string around my arm. My left hand was branded, singed by the lines of the grill which rested on the glowing coals. Everyone stopped talking and turned towards me; I heard gasps. I jumped and pushed away from the hot pit with my right leg before anyone could help.

'I'm fine', I said, wiping the blackness on my left hand on to my clothes with my right arm.

I could smell burnt flesh but felt nothing because the left-sided weakness was still numb. I did not cry or ask for help. My physical asymmetricality, not my visual imbalance, was continually mourned by us all until it gradually improved. At the birthday party, I do not think that I, nor anyone else there, knew that I *had not seen* the barbecue. That's why I fell on top of it.

The LORD opens the eyes of the blind.
The LORD lifts up those who are bowed down.

Psalm 146.8

The Calling

Then one of the seraphs flew to me, holding a live coal that had been taken from the altar with a pair of tongs. The seraph touched my mouth with it and said: 'Now that this has touched your lips, your guilt has departed and your sin is blotted out.' Then I heard the voice of the Lord saying, 'Whom shall I send, and who will go for us?' And I said, 'Here am I; send me!'

Isaiah 6.6–8

The account of Isaiah's vision of service to God is read at each ordination service. Perhaps serendipitously it was a biblical passage I was asked to read in my church at an ordinary Sunday morning service when I was about ten years old. The florid description of the flying winged servants struck me as strange, but Isaiah's confident acceptance of a call for him to step forward and speak, did not. The prophet's eagerness echoed my urge and instinct as a child to step forward and speak – not to speak in the service of God – at least not yet. Rather, I wanted to speak up in order to learn, please and be noticed. Unimaginable things happened to me soon after reading Isaiah's extravagant vision. The malformation in my brain was still unobtrusive then. Unlike the prophet, I was initially silenced and very nearly struck down by a faulty force unleashed in my own body. Awakening after a seizure has claimed me, I normally ask myself, friends, strangers, anyone around me, 'Am I here? Has someone been sent?'

Now the LORD said to Abram, 'Go from your country and from your kindred and your father's house to the land that I will show you.'

Genesis 12.1

Who will I Be?

There is constant movement in the Old Testament. We see the people of Israel hearing God's call, following it, forgetting it, remembering it and living lives rooted in it. Responding to God's call to engage with him is Israel's vocation. Christ is the fulfilment of Israel's vocation. Through Jesus it is revealed that God's call is not only confined to the people of Israel; the sound of God's cry and the feel of God's breath breaks boundaries and borders all over the world.

We see again and again in the Old Testament how God's call to live differently is heard, obeyed and lived out. Jacob encounters God in the form of an angel while crossing the desert alone; he brutally wrestles with God there, leaving him with a limp (Genesis 32.22–31). Being called by God to his service is a struggle; it can be as painful as it is bizarre.

We might see our experience of illness as a calling in reverse: we are hurt, dislocated, stunned, and look beyond our body to discover God's purpose for it. Our sick bodies are God's instruments calling us, nudging us, especially when it hurts. Our bodies are prophetic.

Prophets like Isaiah are called by God to urge people to remember God. Prophets are also called to individually remember who they are in relation to God: they are each set apart to do the work of God. In return, prophets urge people to return to the heart of God so that God's gifts of freedom and purpose may be bestowed on them. Mostly, prophets are unlikely people who are singled out, spoken to and asked to speak up for God. The prophet Jeremiah writes about his own experience of God calling him:

> Now the word of the LORD came to me saying,
>   'Before I formed you in the womb I knew you,
>   and before you were born I consecrated you;
>   I appointed you a prophet to the nations.'
> Then I said, 'Ah, Lord GOD! Truly I do not know how to speak,
> for I am only a boy.' But the LORD said to me,
>   'Do not say, "I am only a boy";
>   for you shall go to all to whom I send you,
>   and you shall speak whatever I command you.
>   Do not be afraid of them,
>   for I am with you to deliver you,
>   says the LORD.'

Jeremiah 1.4–8

Jeremiah tries desperately to understand why he was born as one set apart to be a prophet. Prophets like Jeremiah could be helpful models for those of us with a disability or health problem. Our bodies, however they are formed, make us distinctive. In contrast to the world's obsession with perfection and strength these ideals are by no means prerequisites in order for anyone to speak out on God's behalf.

The opportunity to hear, respond and then embody God's voice is a template for the Christian life. Christ's call is for us to follow him and be conformed to his likeness. The 12 disciples are models and guides, not special helpers, not teacher's pets. Christ speaks to everyone, not to a chosen few. Just as Christ is called out to the wilderness, so are those who follow him. Luke tells us that Jesus leaves the enthusiastic crowds who are keen to hear and see more of him and climbs into Simon's fishing boat. 'Put out into the deep water and let down your nets for a catch,' he says (Luke 5.4). The metaphoric venturing out into the dangerous unknown in order to be fruitful in Jesus' name is more direct in John's account of Jesus' call to Simon. Here, Simon sees Jesus and his curiosity is awakened. 'Where are you staying?' he asks Jesus. He and Andrew want to walk beside him. 'Come and see,' Jesus answers them; it is a beguiling temptation. They followed Jesus and 'remained with him that day' (John 1.39).

Mary is inarguably the ultimate respondent to God when she is greeted by a messenger, Gabriel. Her 'here I am' inaugurates another new way to reply to God. By saying yes to God's invitation to bear God's gift of the Word made flesh, Mary helps God make a new Way, forging a new kingdom and a new Israel. In the long and winding Way to follow God which was first offered for Abraham to walk in, she treads a fresh path into an expansive new world. Gabriel's invitation for Mary to bear God's Son is a bewildering surprise, yet it is aligned with God's former initiatives to call people closer to him. Mary can see this; she seems to know about God's strange yet ultimately glorious ways.

Mary's willing participation in God's enterprise opens up a new way to hear, follow and draw near to God. Mary does so in her body, co-creating Christ with God. Mary travels to visit her cousin who is pregnant with John, the forerunner to her son. John leaps in Elizabeth's womb; it is a movement prefiguring his unsettled and unsettling existence. God's cosmic will, to be radically revealed afresh, races through these women's veins.

Gabriel's parting words to Mary are, 'nothing will be impossible with God' (Luke 1.37). This could be the most appropriate maxim for those who are struggling to connect their sick and hampered bodies with God's will and God's Way. It can be troubling to admit though – especially for those trying to hang on to belief in God – that some things may actually be impossible. Can we dare voice that question? I think we must be honest. Another legitimate question to ask is, 'What does impossible mean?' If we resign our bodies to be forever failing things then we shut ourselves out of God's reach. Some people who are sick may well choose to abandon God, yet we must remember that God never goes away, God waits to welcome or be welcomed at every moment. God is always involved in our journey of recovery. It is in our wandering way through recovery that impossibilities can lead to possibilities which we would not have met had we remained in one place, endlessly mourning our losses with covered up ears and eyes.

Where am I Going?

Encounters with something great – something godly – create unforgettable, if not irrevocable change. Many biblical figures who encounter God are given new names symbolizing a new existence. Their response to God gives them each a new identity: Abram becomes Abraham, Jacob becomes Israel, Sara becomes Sarah, Simon becomes Peter, Saul becomes Paul. The old self is sloughed away, yet the new self is not presented as a finished product because we are all never truly complete. The greatest followers of God's call have been immortalized and mythologized by tradition and it is easy to keep them boxed into history as though that was a time when God clearly did act and call and lead. Stories are still being told though and billions go untold. Our vocation may not have the time-honed contours of the biblical fathers and mothers – but they are no less crucial.

The new person who emerges following illness is less easy to discern. The next stage requires movement away from the old self, developing a new way of being and living. Many people presume that the question, 'How should I live?' must never be posed. Tragically, some never have a choice about how they may live, in places of war and poverty, for instance. Others know that the question is there but lack the bravery to ask it.

A deformed or reformed body presents new limitations, and changes in everyday life often have to be implemented. These can range from acquiring a new bed, to having to move to a new house in a strange place so the wheelchair fits through the door. There is nothing more mundane than needing a toilet fitted on the ground floor, but little may be more important. Limitations are very unfashionable: we privilege self-sufficiency above everything else. Some of us never had the freedom or agency to decide how we live: we have followed our parents' wishes, stayed close to home and done what we were told. Others push against constraint, forging choices for themselves.

When accident or illness strikes we are stopped in our tracks; we aren't going anywhere. Our stricken bodies and our pain can derail or halt our journey. But there is a time to start to move on. It can be lonely and slow. Each attempt is a test, an opportunity to trip up and fail and try again.

As we begin to recover we need to step forward, limping like Jacob, and construct a quest that suits the state of our minds, our means and our bodies. It may well be easier to stay at home, but our scarred bodies have been placed on a threshold now, a cusp that is both burden and springboard, a new beginning and a new end.

This is exposing and risky. Where is God here? Where is the voice, still, small or thunderous calling us out, telling us exactly what to do? A vocation is called out by God to everyone. For those who experience a serious illness, the sound is first heard in the groaning of pain, the weeping that wells up from sorrow. That is the sound we need to listen to even though we are the ones making the sounds. If we are Christ's body, what is it crying out for us to be now that it has been disfigured like Jesus' own body which was pinned to a cross as torture? The vocation of an ill person is to be inspired by listening to his or her body and make way for God to breathe in it. This is the meaning of *inspiration*.

Am I Nearly There?

He who would valiant be 'gainst all disaster,
Let him in constancy follow the Master.
There's no discouragement shall make him once relent
His first avowed intent to be a pilgrim.

John Bunyan, 'To Be a Pilgrim'

John Bunyan's pilgrim has a tenacious purpose: to reach a fixed destination bravely, for the sake of the Lord Almighty. Certainly, knowing where we are going, and why, offers encouragement and promotes speed, as with Bunyan's plucky traveller. Discovering how to live when we are recalibrating how to be me with a harmed body or mind is a puzzle we have to both create and test. Like those scriptural figures, we don't have a fixed end point. There is nothing to be won or snatched. We have to spend time wandering. But this is not a desert; the desert has been crossed. This is a place where we discover and test our limitations using the strange new freedom our illness has opened for us.

The nomad's way of life can help us make sense of what God and our bodies may say to us. A nomad is one who roams freely seeking pasture and nourishment. A nomad has no goal but lives on the lookout for fresh life. A nomad wanders, alert to what might be new and good for her. She is unfettered by possessions and – with verve – lives by grace alone. A nomad proceeds by no assured programme so her life is precarious; she is vulnerable, her risky existence consists of steps in a way that creates a path, rather than follows it. Why? Because the road less travelled offers richer, albeit more precarious resources. God's grace assures a path and love leads the Way.

Although a defined destination is not a nomad's fixation, she takes care to keep a distance from the crowds so as not to be absorbed in the immediate, which may prove barren and fruitlessly distracting.

Now the Lord is the Spirit, and where the Spirit of the Lord is, there is freedom.

2 Corinthians 3.17

A nomad is an unfettered outsider who is unattached to the certainties of power and status. This often invites derision, so a nomad has to become an original thinker, which may invite healthy attention, even intrigue. The nomad is free to look in the faces of others without arrogance or envy, but by opting out of the fixed, straight way her way of life provokes finger-pointing accusations.

Jesus drew crowds, thousands wanted to listen to him and touch him, but he was neither successful nor popular if we measure it by the standards the mainstream world lives by. He was drawn to the edges and never the centre.

Veering off towards a new and unknown path may feel risky but our bodies that have been changed by illness are now forcing us to question what is normal and what we really need to do with our lives now. However, the true purpose of our calling is not only for ourselves because living out a vocation always points beyond ourselves. Our bodies become signposts of God and signs of God in the world.

✠

'Your mother and your brothers are standing outside, wanting to see you.' But [Jesus] said to them, 'My mother and my brothers are those who hear the word of God and do it.'

Luke 8.20–21

Jesus Christ never conformed; he left his home and never returned; he was not a family man. Like a nomad he did not seek fresh pasture, instead he sought to bring fresh life and abundance. Ignoring cultural and political boundaries he ventured into barren and hostile land, telling stories, attracting attention, drawing people to him. Tender and harsh, exposed and illusive, Jesus' mobility exploded peoples' presumptions of morality, safety, love and holiness. John tells us that Jesus promises eternal springs of living water to the Samaritan woman at the well whose drudgery is to seek water as part of her chaotic life. Though she is marginalized by her gender and race Jesus asks her for a drink, allowing her to refresh him (John 4.7–26). This tale encapsulates the essence of vocation.

Jesus feeds thousands before sundown for those who stayed out to listen to him. He transforms water into wine. His generosity makes him popular. It is only when his behaviour is interpreted as an 'unpredictable lifestyle' which threatens to overwhelm those who claim the right to control citizens and impose strict religious law that Jesus ceases to wander. He turns his free direction of travel and resolves to face Jerusalem. Jesus has a fixed destination now: Jerusalem, where first he will be handed over to those with power, and then willingly commend himself to the Father who sent him.

I am Here

> See, my servant shall prosper;
>   he shall be exalted and lifted up,
>   and shall be very high.
> Just as there were many who were astonished at him
>   – so marred was his appearance, beyond human semblance,
>   and his form beyond that of mortals –
> so he shall startle many nations;
>   kings shall shut their mouths because of him;
> for that which had not been told them they shall see,
>   and that which they had not heard they shall contemplate.
>
> Isaiah 52.13–15

Jesus the Word made flesh pitches his tent among us. John uses the Greek verb *skenoo*, which we often translate as 'dwelt' (New

Revised Standard Version), or 'made his home' (Revised English Bible). By losing this metaphor of the tent we overlook the fragility of God's act of sending Jesus as a child to poor parents in the provinces.

Jesus Christ the nomad offers refreshment, rather than seeks it for himself. He does not ask for bread, but offers it. He spends himself for others who are weak and his generosity is limitless. It is crucial to keep remembering that Jesus is a person who resists power and authority at every turn. In Jesus, God who is fullness in every way our minds can fill, becomes empty. God among us is skin and bone; poor, exposed and defenceless. At the end of his life Jesus submits to groups of people for whom self-mastery is life's goal. Jesus resists evil by being there and allowing people to do things to him. This is not unlike a sick person who must submit to the authority of others and let go of autonomy in order to stay alive. Walking in the Way of Christ gives the sick person a head start.

Jesus' Way of love is not pragmatic or necessarily sensible, but it is always authentic. Nothing is held back, nothing is saved – 'just in case'. False love retains a modicum of detachment; control is preserved and limitations are kept in check, however faint they may seem. By contrast, Jesus is pure and selfless love which often takes the form of service to others.

At the Last Supper Jesus washes his disciples' feet, much to their horror and astonishment. This act is more than a friendly gesture, it is also a symbol of servanthood. By kneeling down at their dirty feet with a towel around his waist he prepares his friends for the time – only hours away – when his body will be offered as a complete sacrifice of love. Sometimes the absurdity of humility can seem too strange for us to contemplate, but perfect love is like that. A life lived for others in weakness may not be an attractive offer. So why would we want to follow Jesus who allows his whole self to be possessed, mocked and become an 'it'?

From the moment Paul was converted by Christ to follow him and teach the world about him he became a nomad, travelling far beyond Jewish land. Paul grasped the worldly foolishness of God's new Way of love and immediately renounced power. He also risked his life and offered himself as an object of hatred.

Importantly, he never loses sight of his old ways, nor forgets his old name. In fact, it becomes a shadow side he uses creatively for both himself and for those to whom he is writing. Paul tries to banish his pride and become a servant, a nomad and a fool. He makes it very clear in his first letter to the people in Corinth:

> Where is the one who is wise? Where is the scribe? Where is the debater of this age? Has not God made foolish the wisdom of the world? For since, in the wisdom of God, the world did not know God through wisdom, God decided, through the foolishness of our proclamation, to save those who believe. For Jews demand signs and Greeks desire wisdom, but we proclaim Christ crucified, a stumbling-block to Jews and foolishness to Gentiles, but to those who are the called, both Jews and Greeks, Christ the power of God and the wisdom of God. For God's foolishness is wiser than human wisdom, and God's weakness is stronger than human strength.
>
> 1 Corinthians 1.20–25

The Suffering Servant

At first, the prophet Isaiah's keen messenger has lips on fire ready to serve and speak in the service of God. Later though, the servant is a suffering servant, too sick to actively work or even speak. Prefiguring Christ on the cross, this servant is endlessly compassionate, not least by visibly remaining there, immobilized and absorbent with pain and objectification. Now his wounds cry out and his humble silence deafens those who can be bothered to notice him.

> He was oppressed, and he was afflicted,
>   yet he did not open his mouth;
> like a lamb that is led to the slaughter,
>   and like a sheep that before its shearers is silent,
>   so he did not open his mouth.
>
> Isaiah 53.7

Watching and listening for signs and sounds of God is required of us all, even when what we see before us may not be pleasant. Experiences of illness, physical pain and discomfort invite us to discover, perhaps for the first time, that God is not only present in pretty places. Fullness of life means different things now that our bodies are different; and because it sometimes does not at first make much sense it has to be constantly reinterpreted and our mind and our senses need to be reattuned. In order to discern a new vocation for our bodies we must use the unsettledness that our illness has caused us.

The selflessness of Jesus – the one who pitched his tent and was pinned to a cross – may seem at odds with the endless politeness that is often required of a priest. People seem to want vicars to be preferably male, posh, pale, charming, clever, witty and strong, but where can the suffering body of Jesus be seen there? Jesus was never a personality; he drew attention to himself by much stranger means.

There will be time, there will be time
To prepare a face to meet the faces that you meet;
T. S. Eliot, 'The Love Song of Alfred J. Prufrock'

Jesus never prepared a face because his authentic love made him transparent. Christians, and priests in particular, are called to be servants of God. Clergy must turn their eyes towards both God and the world, which is not always easy. When someone senses a call to be a priest they offer themselves as a sign and focus of the mysterious interplay between human and divine life. Clergy must be rooted in prayer rather than success and business. Prayer, busy-ness rather than productivity, consumes their time.

The Servant Priest

Priests have to accept that their call involves entering into the Way of life of a nomad. Most will probably face derision at some point, will lose friends, become an unknown known wherever they go, attracting attention, suspicion and repulsion. Yet all Christians – not just priests – move on in their lives in communion with the body of Christ which we understand and receive as the Church. Acts laid down by Christ, such as the Last Supper and washing feet, are copied in church; work such as serving the poor, sitting with those who are unpopular or unfashionable is done in attempts to become more like him.

There is normally little to show for a life lived as a servant of God. Time can feel wasted, we can feel spent and used and our identities are often censored either by ourselves or those we aim to serve. The burden of humility and poverty can sometimes disfigure those who, one summer afternoon in a packed cathedral at an ordination service, knelt before a bishop and promised to be transformed into the likeness of Christ through prayer, obedience and servanthood. But the lure of power, wealth and success is compulsive and difficult to ignore. Some clergy hold fast to their calling and they are very admirable, faithful priests. R. S. Thomas's poem, 'Country Clergy', offers an unromantic reflection on the lonely, humble and foolishly wise commitment some priests offer.

Country Clergy

I see them working in old rectories
By the sun's light, by candlelight,
Venerable men, their black cloth
A little dusty, a little green
With holy mildew. And yet their skulls,
Ripening over so many prayers,
Toppled into the same grave
With oafs and yokels. They left no books,
Memorial to their lonely thought
In grey parishes; rather they wrote
On men's hearts and in the minds
Of young children sublime words
Too soon forgotten. God in his time
Or out of time will correct this.

R. S. Thomas

A priest who is blind and must be led to the altar points to the God who draws close to us in order that we may truly see with our heart; a priest who limps up the aisle reveals the will of God to greet, grapple and challenge us; a priest whose face is darkened by depression invites us to see the sorrowful face of Christ in the garden of Gethsemane. We are all called to be conformed to Christ and we should all become icons as we are, not glossy posters of who we want to be one day. A perfect priest, a perfect Christian, is an idol.

I Will Be Who I Will Be

Getting better does not mean going back, neither does moving on mean forgetting who we once were. A nomad is not homeless, but home takes on new meanings. Mobility does not define how fast we can walk, but how freely we can sit with strangers. God waits and walks with us at every moment.

We each have vocations. Whether it is as a priest, a mother, a teacher or poet, each calling is an opportunity to transform the world, however insignificant it may seem. Testing and living out a vocation should not involve taking on a heavy yoke. Although it might not be easy, the challenge should be liberating and exciting. Recovering from illness is a good opportunity to think more creatively about what God can do with us in the world now that things are different for us. Paradoxically, it is when our world seems to be dark and bewildering when we see things more clearly.

The voice of one responding to God's call says, 'Here I am! – yes all right – I'll give it a go.' But this doesn't mean that we will never ask God in a moment of despair, 'Where are you?' Both cries: 'Here I am!' and 'Where are you?' are not mutually exclusive at all but haunting and very real. Muscular and unswervingly confident Christianity can be a mere performance because doubt and fear have their place, especially when we are trying to make sense of how to live following an illness or trauma. The word 'hosanna' might help us here. It is used repeatedly on Palm Sunday when the drama of Jesus entering into Jerusalem on a donkey is re-enacted in churches all over the world. The congregation shout 'hosanna!'

mimicking those who welcomed Jesus as their new king and Saviour. The triumphant cries of those greeting Jesus soon died out; the crowd wanted a great king so Jesus' quiet powerlessness was an affront to them. They did not hear Jesus' darker calls to those who patiently hung on his every word before he became so popular. This familiar Hebrew word, *hosanna*, is easy to take for granted because it is heard in prayers many times, including every Eucharist service. But *hosanna* is not simply a foreign word for 'hurrah!' The root meaning in Hebrew of *hosanna* is in fact a plea for help, a desperate appeal for deliverance. In that one word, a cry of desperation can blossom, like Christ's risen body, and become a hymn of praise.

May it be upon that word our own stories are grounded.

I shall not die, but I shall live,
    and recount the deeds of the LORD.

Psalm 118.17

6

People

I normally arrived at church alone and early on Sunday mornings, round the side door. In the choir vestry wardrobe was my own hanger with a red cassock and a white surplice; the ruffs were shared and that went on first. The members of the choir at St John the Baptist, Baxenden, were all female so our sound was unbalanced, but not without gusto. There were five other girls around the age of ten. But one singer, Betty, was in her eighties. Between songs her mouth was tight with consternation, not when we giggled at Tuesday evening choir practices, but mostly at the choice of hymns. Our hymn book was very modern: *Mission Praise*. There was a collective groan among the youth when we were asked to turn to the older hymn book – 'Ancient and Prehistoric' we called it, rather than its real title, *Hymns Ancient & Modern*.

Mrs Lomas, a teacher at our attached primary school, was in charge of the choir; she gently introduced new Christian music. We sang modern songs in daily school assemblies too. The vicar's daughter was the church organist. I was second tambourine, under the tutelage of Mrs Grimes who was our school caretaker.

Many of the songs and hymns we sang are still alive under my skin. Years later I realized that some songs were psalms set to music, or poetry from the Old Testament prophets. Some songs told stories from the Gospels, others were derived from narratives in the Old Testament. None of the songs seemed to focus on the cross, on the suffering of Christ, nor relied on the contemporary evangelical obsession with Jesus' blood making everything better. Each song was joyful and *fun*. Many were also relentlessly upbeat and that was the only thing about God I knew.

One of my favourites was 'Jubilate', which had a Jewish tune and feel – not that I had ever heard Jewish music nor met a Jewish person. I had no idea what 'jubilate' meant, or what language it came from, neither did I realize that the lyrics come directly from Psalm 100:

Make a joyful noise to the LORD, all the earth.
  Worship the LORD with gladness;
  Come into his presence with singing.

Psalm 100.1–2

Those of us in the choir used to dance to it on the red carpeted platform at the end of the aisle, giving the long-suffering congregation an energetic performance before we rushed off to Sunday school across the road.

I loved Sunday school, and later, Pathfinders, which was the church version of secondary school. Paper pamphlets were completed in the name of education, I suppose. In the summer we went on adventure days out with other churches in the area. There was drama, sport, craft, in the name of fun. Was Jesus in the fun and the friendliness? Surely. But I did not understand who Jesus was, what Jesus was, so how could I lose him, find him, or be found by him?

I owned a pristine copy of the Good News Bible. Its yellow cover with a rainbow motif was never opened. We had Scripture classes at school. More art class than a theology lesson, we drew arks on sugar paper and glued tissue flowers on to drawings of the garden of the wise man who built his house upon the rocks. There was no attempt to connect rocks to God, or prayer. God was 'out there', not 'right here'. Nothing was said about the relationship God desired to have with those he made in his image. The stories that we told, sung and danced to seemed to be self-contained – from nowhere, going nowhere; but were offered by God to provide enlightening entertainment.

Jesus was a man. I think *that is it*. Jesus was a friendly teacher with special powers and so we should be happy about it and have *fun* together and be friends too. Any element of judgement was eradicated; sin was absent; stubbornness and sadness did not exist. Death was also absent. Going to church made us nicer.

There was very little liturgy at church. Services had no structure, young people were not admitted to communion until their teens, and children were sent out to Sunday school after a few worship songs and did not return. There was a monthly family service but it was normally a drama we rushed together and performed in place of the sermon.

Worship had no shape; praise had neither means nor end. God the Holy Trinity was not to be encountered, adored, prostrated or knelt before, reached out or bowed to, or processed towards. The late Victorian church had virtually no symbols to make up visually what was lacking theologically and sacramentally.

I did not know about the Holy Spirit. God's gentle force was not offered as a go-between, a possibility, or an intimate means of revelation. I expected nothing from God and expected that God expected nothing from me. Transcendence, mystery, beauty; silence, ritual and glory; feasts, festivals, saints. These words were unknown words and traditions.

God was everywhere and nowhere.

Lex orandi, lex credendi, which can loosely be translated as 'what we pray is what we believe', is at the heart of Anglican theology and practice. Our prayers at once teach us and tell us; we pray in order to learn, we learn so that we might pray more. The more we pray, the more we know; the more we pray the more we realize we do not know and so on and so on in an unending flow and interchange between theology and worship.

Primary school assembly every day included two hymns, a homily from the head teacher, and prayers, including the Lord's Prayer. We chanted grace before and after lunch. *For what we are about to/have received may the Lord make us truly thankful. Arrrmen.* We prayed in the classroom at 3.30 before home time, thanking God for our day at school.

Reflecting on this now it was a disembodied, passive, even begrudging reminder to behave. 'The Lord' could be a title for one of the landed gentry living a few miles north in the Ribble Valley. I don't think I connected God to creation, to Christ, to the nativity, crucifixion or the resurrection. Jesus' breaking of bread with people he met on the road to Emmaus, Jesus eating broiled fish with his bewildered friends, the sound of sheer silence that Elijah heard when he encountered God on Mount Horeb (1 Kings 19.11–18), the Last Supper in the upper room, the manna falling from the sky: not one of these narratives and signs had gone deep enough in my heart or head for me to connect them to the sentences we mumbled daily. Faith requires multiple, ceaseless connections. Teaching anyone anything is the art of opening doors. The gift of Christ expands the connections we can make to God exponentially.

> Lift up your heads, O gates!
>   and be lifted up, O ancient doors!
>   that the King of glory may come in.
>
> Psalm 24.7

Theology is the act of creating systems, linking mystery to logic, history to philosophy, Scripture to literature. Lack of it left me with baggy and benign instruction about life and God. As a student I had violin lessons offered free by Lancashire County Council. I wanted to learn to play the violin because I wanted to learn *anything*. I only knew one person who played an instrument and it was a flute. I had never been to a classical music concert – I didn't know they existed. I wonder how different my approach to learning the violin would have been if I had heard a Bach partita, or been to a concert, or even seen someone playing it on TV.

I am ashamed and confused when I reflect on how little I learned about God as a child. Did I have such meagre curiosity? It exposes an absence of expectation that I am angry about now. Or perhaps my brain damage has erased it all.

Churchgoing as a child has not left me with guilt which aches like a bad tooth for life. It has not left me with a manic baulking at an omniscient judge. The Bible was not used as a tool or weapon against me. I am very thankful for my time at St. John's. Despite the vicar being male, the church was a very female environment, a loving place where I had many friends. *I enjoyed it.* Perhaps that is how God is best revealed. I was loved, shown love, and learned to love.

Many years later I discovered the eleventh-century theologian Anselm of Canterbury's explanation of what theology is: *fides quarens intellectum*, which means 'faith searching for understanding'. His argument about the healthy contributions of philosophy when trying to understand the existence of God made absolute sense to me and offered a gift of relief. It is love, he states, and interest in God that seeks a deeper understanding and knowledge of God. As I lacked the latter, the former waned and weakened, but the love of and interest in God did not die completely. I eventually found God and God found me.

When I was ill the first time I did not pray, though many people prayed *for* me. They kept telling me so, and I admit that their desperate assurances helped me feel connected and remembered. I imagined and believed that through their prayers my pain and trauma were not confined to my body, nor to the hospital, nor my parents. I was told repeatedly that I was being prayed for at Blackburn Cathedral, which made me feel special. It reassured me more deeply that this harrowing I was undergoing was being housed in a large holy place and held by others; this horror was being portioned out like bitter pills for others to taste too. No one claimed that God would save me; no one whispered in my ear that God would make everything better. When pain and fear and sorrow broke into me so quickly, there was no space for God to be noticed and known. There was no structure built in my heart and mind to help me connect my pain to the pain of Christ. The experience of terror made no room for God. It is quite obvious now for me to see that every 'hello', every touch, stroke or offering of a wet sponge to suck when I was not allowed to drink or eat before surgery was a prayer, a revelation of Christ, an act of thanksgiving, and the work of praise. Therefore, such blindness meant that recovery was revealed by being happy again, going back to church, forgetting about the pain and the fear and the reality of death. There were many more songs to learn.

Jubilate Deo!

My great grandmother Hannah Cardwell (née Wilson) died when I was 12. She had married a Roman Catholic and her children, including my paternal grandmother, were brought up as Roman Catholics. There were rosaries and kitsch pictures of Mary on shelves and a plywood dresser in the living room of her council house in Haslingden, another small post-cotton mill closure ghost town where I lived until I was six, and where my grandmother lived until her death in 2015 at the age of 85. She died in the two-bedroom council house in which my dad was born. I used to visit my great-grandmother's house regularly with my mum. The house stank of dogs and tobacco. My Uncle Bob, her youngest of seven, was illiterate, unmarried, and lived with her all his life. Stepping into the house was like being in another country. I was always fearful and fascinated.

A large group of men in white shirts and black ties were smoking, coughing and talking nervously outside St Mary's Catholic Church, Haslingden. I walked into the church and before me, in the dim light, was my great grandmother dressed and laid out in an open coffin. The church smelt sweet. There were pictures and pastel coloured statues everywhere. Gold gilded the walls and pillars along the neo-Gothic nave. The building was founded in 1859, 21 years before St John's, Baxenden. White lilies spilt over the white marble altar and on to the pristine sanctuary. Candles were nervously flickering beside the coffin on tall candlesticks. I stepped forward. It was the first dead body I had ever seen. Her face was shiny and its uncompromising stillness dared me to move closer. Strangers who were related to me were walking towards the coffin, bending towards her clothed body and kissing her forehead. I followed them, stepped nearer, bowed my head and pressed my lips to her face. The stone slab chill still lingers on my lips.

Foundations, Rocks and Broken Stones

> He drew me up from the desolate pit,
> out of the miry bog,
> and set my feet upon a rock,
> making my steps secure.
>
> Psalm 40.2

When someone is suddenly sick it can feel as though violence has been inflicted and imposed upon a body. The tender body is broken apart and it can become a gruesome drama, even if the violence is taking place under the skin. Those who have nurtured, created and desired that body are cleared away from it – as though it is a health hazard – and are forced to make way for professional rescuers to work on scene within the area of conflict.

The sick human body fights with itself and those who love can only watch this enfleshed combat like an audience unaware of the plot. The body they visit or sit beside becomes almost unknown: papery, fragile and still, not like the gentle state of sleep, but stony stiff as though never once fruitful. Skin is covered in tasteless and multi-coloured fabric. The extent of nakedness seems endless. A formula is easily figured out: the greater the exposure of flesh, the greater the prospect of death.

When a child is sick it can feel as though she has been abducted from her parents. Against instinct she must be handed over to people who know better. The parent is taken hostage, stripped – it feels at first – not only of their child, but of their entitlement: mother, father, mummy, daddy. Their precious fruits are picked and seized because they are at risk of being gobbled up by death. Soon though, in watching, waiting, gazing and praying, her motherhood, his fatherhood, becomes mysteriously transfigured, and the soul, blood and bones of them are for ever marked by these experiences. Sleep will never be smooth and seamless again. Memories of the child's miniature body at birth resurface: it was once supple, spongy and slippery. They recall, breathless with panic, their newborn that at first was only a breath in and breath out away from expiry. The eerie life drive which once electrified their hands when they held their baby is now remembered in cool, wrinkling, empty hands that shake and wring with sorrow.

The hospital dictates rules and routines. Time is not kept by the sun but is marked by staff changes, tea trolleys, cleaning shifts. Light is harsh, it is regulated by manufactured rather than natural rules. Choice is absent; it is only found in the menus with short lists offering boxes to be ticked. Watchers graze, barely eating, losing weight. Hot food, bodily excretions and disinfectant dictate the scent. Privacy is found in flimsy curtains which fail to contain sound; urgent communication is made in faces and whispers. Only get-well-soon cards point back towards home, but the cheery images mock the horrifying reality that home is far off and will never really be home again.

The memory of seeing their green-dun child writhing in a hospital bed like badly shot deer will never completely fade. The consolation of hospital is the air of expertise which comes close in emergency rushes, in jittery groups of trainees. On occasion it is felt as gravitas with the appearance of a consultant. Parents and carers can only watch and wait and long for the experts to just get on and fix the person they love.

The hospital's language is confusing and unsettling for those who don't work there. Many different registers are spoken and written by doctors, nurses, cleaners and even fellow visitors on the ward. The babble of numbers, names and jargon spouted out in the name of communication and information can feel like bombardments. And yet the gaps and silences endured by those who wait quietly beside the hospital bed are equally disturbing. The absence of sound coming from the one they love who lies too still and too soundless is chilling. This emptiness and unknowing that is formed around that bed in contrast to the clamour of the ward will be translated home by parents and child, even if the child recovers well. Their true story can only ever be told in the unspoken language they invented between them in hospital.

God's Ground

> That one is like a man building a house, who dug deeply and laid the foundation on rock; when a flood arose, the river burst against that house but could not shake it, because it had been well built.
>
> Luke 6.48

We build walls presuming that boundaries provide shelter. Privacy and security are prized commodities everywhere. It is easy to deceive ourselves: we try too hard to construct safety. Ultimately we are dust. Like pots made of clay our bodies easily break. Foundations crack and start to show when pain and trauma break in. If the way we walk in fair weather is not grounded in

God, the earth on which we stand when storms gather can feel very unstable. The first act of faith is an acceptance that God created the ground on which we stand as pure gift. We tread a path that is grounded by God. The invitation is to walk in the expectation that it is God's will to encounter us as he did Jacob, Elijah, Simon Peter, Paul, Mary Magdalene. Perhaps slowly, or begrudgingly, we learn that firm foundations are built by thankfulness and prayer.

Prayers attune our senses and help to plant us in a reality that is beyond our own constructing. Watching the suffering and bearing the silence or the cries of someone we love who is ill can render us powerless and also speechless. Yet God was not silenced when those he created turned away from him in the garden, or in the desert, or in exile. God was not silenced by the crucifixion. Further, those he came to serve were not silenced but were given new ways of speaking about God. The roots and rocks from which this language springs is the humble, suffering Christ. God gives us words and structures for our suffering.

Parents: A New Mother Tongue

Suffering unearths new words. Suffering is by no means restricted to the one in pain. Rather, the sufferer, parent, partner, friend construct new forms of communication in order to liaise with themselves, each other and with God: the suffering One; Jesus Christ. The sick body before them may speak new languages in sight, touch, hearing, smell, memory. Parents learn to parse the varied tones, rasps, metres, rhythms and pitches of their baby's cries, decoding what kind of discomfort needs to be alleviated. When serious illness occurs their ill child, whether grown-up or newborn, communicates new needs using desperate methods. If it feels like regression, it is.

New languages are formed at times like these. Parents invent a crash-created dialect of their own that never goes rusty. They also develop a journalistic *commentariat* on the minutiae of the sick body before them. Of course, the doctors are fluent in the language of the body and when they group around their child's bed it sounds like gobbledegook. Parents never pick up this language completely and learn a pigeon version, frantically making informed guesses and translations. This foreign language bamboozles their ears so it is difficult for them to remember what was said once the doctors have rushed away. They are desperate to understand what is being described about their child's body and their child's future but they silence themselves, ashamed and frustrated that they are unable to communicate. Sadly, their instinctual interpretations of what their child's body may be doing and speaking goes unsaid.

Parents are not always certain that the child in the sick bed can hear, so exchanges between the carers are silent and expressed in the face alone. They learn to look into the other's face in a way that reminds them of when they fell in love and learned to gaze. Now their bodies communicate various modes of fear they never knew existed.

Parents also co-create a spiel in order to articulate the child's progress to those beyond the hospital or sickbed. It is a compact language, mostly spoken in the past and present tense – rarely the future. There are few verbs in this repeated and strangely dispassionate package because nothing much happens and nothing much is said. The spiel dulls and drains the speaker with each telling.

The language of silence is the most difficult for parents to learn. Waiting beside the sick becomes an act of contemplation.

Partner: A New Lexicon

The lover of a sick person tries to read the language of her partner's naked body. The lover's language is fresher, less honed by time, less fired by instinct than it is in the language of the parents. The sick body before the partner is not a desirable object of pleasure now. Instead, it is one to be watched, cleaned, waited on and waited for. The intimacy of the body here is not reciprocal. We can read in the lover's patient gaze a desire to alleviate; the lover diagnoses pain and discomfort rather than desire and pleasure.

Beside the sickbed her adoration is expressed in tender acts of charity. The beloved's sick body is infantilized and desexualized by its multiple needs. Touch here is not erotic. Rather, the partner touches in order to fix and console.

Love is expressed by patiently *getting things done* at times like these. Surprise is restricted here to eyes opening unexpectedly. Humdrum everyday tasks aren't shared any more. Encouragements are whispered in the hope that the poetry of love will find a voice once the dull drone of aches and pain dies down.

In spite of vows exchanged and legal documents, the lover is free to leave. There is a choice. Relationships are flimsier than blood ties. Marriage, mortgage, unspoken expectations, can be broken. The person she promised to have and hold may not be the same person any more. The partnership may need to be reinterpreted.

Money may not be as plentiful: illness can seriously impact work and income. Fantasies of God-given roles fade. Spontaneity is planned; pain and petty physical needs, rather than pleasure dominate. The simple orderings of domesticity can quickly turn to drudgery. A new role may be imposed: the servant, the nurse, the mother.

Male or female, the partner has to become a homemaker. The home can feel like a safe or suffocating fortress and particular rooms contain specific means of entrapment. The kitchen becomes a wearying place for fuel-making; it is no longer a place of chatter of the day or the preparation of a good meal to be shared slowly. The dinner table is unused and the one who has become The Carer nibbles cold food on the sofa with the television on for distraction, but the sound off so as not to wake the sleeping convalescent. The bedroom is a place of interminable darkness, the bed an over-heated rectangle awaiting another eruption of pain and fear.

Building-Up Bodies

We can never be our own masters and we are unable to rebuild ourselves alone. We need others to contribute to our bodies' recon-struction. It will not be the same as it was before our bodies fell apart; it may not be pretty and it will never be finished. Building ourselves back up requires a variety of gifts and a variety of people.

Our memories are fragmented: odd parts may unexpectedly fit together, while other parts are broken apart or lost. Our bodies tell our stories. When we are absent from our bodies, through unconsciousness, pain or trauma, we may have to rely on others to tell our story. Illness fragments us and breaks us open and our bodies contain fissures, scars, cracks and ruptures.

Those who love and care for us can help piece us back together, but it can be difficult to guess how much we should allow others to share in the work of making us well. Our bodies may be used as fragments in their own illness narratives too. Our stories become collages, inseparable from those we believe are entirely our own. Those with neat and smooth stories mistakenly presume that theirs are superior. But the fewer the fissures and absences, the greater the risk of a predictable, isolated life. Our identity is fractured and incomplete and we often learn slowly and stubbornly to be thankful for that.

The Rock of Our Salvation

'I will be standing there in front of you on the rock at Horeb. Strike the rock, and water will come out of it, so that the people may drink.' Moses did so, in the sight of the elders of Israel.

Exodus 17.6

In the book of Exodus Moses strikes the rock and water rushes out. Life pours out from the rugged stone. God is tested by the people of Israel and once again God gives life. Surely this is the ultimate test? The greatest sign of new life is the resurrection of Jesus and it is freely given, not requested or expected. Our problems often start when we think that abundance and ease are signs of God's blessing. Yet God is most keen, most able where power is absent and humiliation is present.

And the rock was Christ.

1 Corinthians 10.4

Jesus rejects power when the devil invites him to turn stones to bread. Jesus is famished yet does not manipulate his abilities to satiate his desire. He deprives himself: he that is the sign of God's plenty chooses emptiness and suffers in solidarity with people who are hungry for bread and justice. Jesus undergoes deprivation. Those stones that Jesus rejects return when a woman accused of adultery is threatened with death by stoning (John 8.1–11). The accusers put down their rocks when they realize that the stones they clutch represent their lust for power. Shamefully, they knew that by aiming them at a voiceless woman they were projecting their own shame. The stones in their hands were their hard hearts. Following Jesus' crucifixion, the stone rolled away from the tomb is a beating but broken heart.

> The earth shook, and the rocks were split.
>
> Matthew 27.51

Jesus always resists control. He does not retaliate towards those who seek to mock and control him. He openly 'set his face to go to Jerusalem' (Luke 9.51). This is the face that Isaiah foresees will be 'set like flint' (Isaiah 50.7) among those who long to gouge out his exposed flesh. At his trial Jesus embraces pain. Human violence ruptures the contours of his body and the sweating flesh of Christ relents to brutal human force. Earth breaks open, rocks tear apart in response, and so a new world order is unleashed through his death.

A dark, chilled tomb created by scooped out earth was Jesus' resting place. The silent Word – a cool and stiffening body – was carried by grieving friends and carefully placed into the yawning mouth of The End. The lips of the tomb were sealed with a boulder, yet death did not have the last word; death could not silence God. Out of the rock the Word re-enfleshed gives us new ways of speaking about our bodies and our terror. Therefore, through Christ's resurrection we are invited to become living, speaking stones. We are given new ways of speaking about ourselves to others and to God.

✠

Jesus' death doesn't end the story; it opens up a new one. Hopefully, in time, we will be able to say this about our own suffering. Although there may be many things that have changed in our bodies and in our lives, this should not force us to erase the memories of who we were before the pain began. Our suffering doesn't need to be isolated from the past and the scars on our bodies can sit alongside the suffering flesh of Christ. The humiliation of being touched and wiped by strangers, and crying with pain in front of people we have never met before is ennobled by the humiliated Son of God. The pangs of indignity we may feel can be incorporated into our vision of the suffering of God if our imagination is bold enough.

A new heart I will give you, and a new spirit I will put within you; and I will remove from your body the heart of stone and give you a heart of flesh.

Ezekiel 36.26

If we dare, our illnesses may open out new connections to new people and places. The suffering body, whether it be seen or felt, can become a catalyst for new relationships. These relationships often gain momentum outside the home – reaching beyond the confines of families. Roles change and we may realize that our old roles don't fit any more. We learn to speak new languages to new people. Although this might be uncomfortable at first, it can be liberating. Very little is as fixed and stable as we would like it to be. We learn this bit by bit as we recover and try to adjust to change.

Church: The Broken Body of Christ

God wants our stories to be shared. We can reclaim them, and as we begin to tell our stories of coping with illness and pain to others we start to enlarge and enrich them by including them into a larger story – that is, the story of Christ's suffering and his resurrection. If our suffering can create living stones, we can build a living body of Christ. This is not to build a monument of triumph, nor a historical artefact, but rather a fragile, messy, distorted and glorious body. The broken Body of Christ is handed over to us. It is God's offering of himself.

This body is called the Church and Christ is the cornerstone. We distort the Church most often when we blindly deny our own feelings of frailty and fear. The solid rock always seems much safer than the fragmented, half-living bony stones and shards that we really know we are made of, but this is an illusion.

This idea may not easily align with our cliché ideas of church with its pale choir boys in starched choir ruffs; bishops carrying croziers with bejewelled fingers; polished brass candlesticks held by male hands in a gleaming sanctuary. The perceived spotlessness of the Church can make us afraid of hearing the sound of our own cracking voices and feeling our own shallow breath. Where is the stinking rottenness of our bodies there? How are the sobs and shrieks of pain heard above the *Glorias* played from the organ loft? Where is the interminable dark and silent night found when Sunday morning is heralded by bells rung by unbelieving enthusiasts, rushing off to the next church just as the service is about to start?

'And I tell you, you are Peter, and on this rock I will build my church.'

Matthew 16.18

The fixed stone altar covered in starched linen presided by a priest in embroidered silk vestments may seem completely disconnected from our hospital bed or sickbed at home. The unmade bed and the unopened bills can add further insults to the limitations illness has imposed. Pain, guilt and unremitting reminders of our imperfections add further distance from the Church despite the fact that it is the place in which the narrative of Christ's haphazard birth, his torture and death is retold over and over again. The Eucharist service is the most eloquent expression of God's participation in human suffering, and this service is the lifeblood of the Church. Here we are invited to connect our shattered bodies with Jesus' suffering and resurrected body. The story did not end with suffering and neither does ours. The fractured bread held aloft by the priest at every altar is an epicentre of every quaking heart and broken bone.

'For where two or three are gathered in my name, I am there among them.'

Matthew 18.20

The Church is not a building: it is flawed people tending to sick bodies and fragile minds. The glorious body of Christ is often most alive when its ordinary people serve secretly or behind walls; they become living stones. Living stones learn that suffering in isolation is not life-giving, but sharing in suffering can be. Essential to the Eucharist is the communication of bodies: our bodies and Jesus' body. Extraordinarily, it is here where the divine and the human body coalesce. But first we are asked to communicate with those besides us in the pews. Halfway through the service of Holy Communion the congregation is asked by the celebrant to be at peace with one another, so we shake hands and look into each other's eyes. Some people find this uncomfortable. The flimsy shields we construct around us are broken at this moment and the fragility behind our eyes can sometimes be spotted. For others, it may be the only time in the week when they are touched.

The broken body of Christ is alive when a visit is made to someone whose partner died after long-drawn-out cancer. The body of Christ is alive where a priest anoints a dying man from the alcoholics' hostel who is begging for his mum between his acrid rasps. The broken Body of Christ is alive wherever prayers for the sick are uttered.

Miracle
Not the one who takes up his bed and walks
But the ones who have known him all along
And carry him in

Their shoulders numb, the ache and stoop deeplocked
In their backs, the stretcher handles
Slippery with sweat. And no let-up

Until he's strapped on tight, made tiltable
And raised to the tiled roof, then lowered for healing.
Be mindful of them as they stand and wait

For the burn of the paid-out ropes to cool,
Their slight lightheadedness and incredulity
To pass, those ones who had known him all along.

Seamus Heaney

Seamus Heaney had a stroke in 2005. The great Irish bard was struck down. In his poem, 'Miracle', we see him focus, not on the healed one, but on the ones who, in solidarity and hope, find a way to get their paralysed friend in front of Jesus who has a reputation for healing people. Interestingly, this story is mentioned in all three synoptic Gospels (Matthew, Mark and Luke). Heaney admits that he could not have written this without his experience of being carried into hospital himself. These carriers are strong, ingenious yet physically tested by their efforts to lift the man through the roof; they work as a team. The paralysed man's inconvenient body is freed, but only because he allowed himself to be hoisted up and trusted that the men would not drop him. Courageously, he submits his weakness to the strength of those who love him and hope to help build up his body. Each carrier is desperate to get their friend close to Jesus whose *mysterious* touch is a means of liberation.

Let yourselves be built into a spiritual house.

1 Peter 2.5

Soon after my second haemorrhage the vicar came to visit. I had stopped going church by then though. I was no longer in the choir, no longer playing the violin. Hollins High was a secular school so there were no assemblies, no songs, no hymns, no grace. The vicar wore a long woollen black cloak and spoke with a posh clipped 'accent' unmatched in our patch of Lancashire. He had never been to visit before and he came unannounced, buoyant with assured yet generous purpose. He brought faith in, and with it an unswerving and solid certainty which no one in the house was sure of any more. The extravagant swoosh of his heavy cape when he walked through the door mocked our shaky attempts at recovery and normality. My dad turned off the television and stood up just in time. I offered him the armchair I had been lounging on. Following embarrassed and stilted small talk which cloaked our trauma, he asked if he could pray. Only my father and I were in the room – my mother was making tea. At the moment when the vicar closed his eyes and engaged his well-formed and well-meaning piety, two shell-shocked sufferers jointly acted-out belief, creating a performance which was half-pantomime, half-tragedy.

7

Prayer

At 15, I sat alone for an hour twice a week on the dim and draughty first-floor landing at Hollins School. I had dropped a subject to catch up with school work. At St John's primary – just up the road – I used to be sent out to the landing because I was striding ahead, not lagging behind everybody. Admitting that I should quit a subject following my dramatic epileptic seizure was as humiliating as the attack itself.

I didn't give up French though. It was my second favourite lesson after English, and classes were always held in the afternoon. We sat in pairs learning how to ask where the *syndicat d'initiative* was, and I would stare at the tiled floor, fantasizing about how gentle, how sweet it would be to lie down and sleep there. The floor was like a menacing magnet. My fatigue was weighty, pulling my body downwards using the laws of gravity to demand rest. My brain hurt as though it was overloaded and like a computer needing a reboot to straighten out blips. I didn't think about moving to a different desk that would suit my profound new vision loss because, first, I was unable to see *how* I could not see, and second, I did not understand what strategies I might use to mitigate such loss. I resisted the urge to sleep on the hard floor that my body was desperate to lie on in the same way I denied the invisible absence of vision.

I was one of the lucky few to be chosen to do a GCSE in media studies at the further education college a mile down the road; it was a new and uncharacteristic initiative for our school. Every Wednesday morning I got to wear my own clothes and rubbed shoulders with older teenagers, though I didn't ever speak to any of them. I watched them, observing their freedom. In the class we learned how to promote records, write scripts and prepare story-boards for soap operas. Media studies was not an academic subject in the formal sense but I was asked to create ideas of my own and required to connect to the world beyond Accrington. For two years, after the media studies class I caught the bus – not back to school but straight home, skipping PE and maths, and no one ever seemed to notice. When I turned up to maths on the other days I stared at the stark and beautiful symbols on the page but failed to grasp what I was supposed to do with them. My brain could no longer find patterns and remember rules. I ended up with a D in maths, in sharp contrast to my A in media studies.

'I wonder how water cools down?' I asked my friend Susan as we watched crystals melt in a petri dish in chemistry class.

'We learned that in physics while you were away Jennie,' she said.

Sitting in the back row of science classes three times a week was like watching daytime TV in black and white, in Russian, with the sound down low. I got an F in science GCSE. Religious studies was two years of colouring in and petty ethical enquiry of 'issues' tenuously related to three of the four Gospels. I got an A, but remember nothing about it apart from the time when the local conservative MP, Ken Hargreaves, came to talk to us about the evils of abortion. I got two As in English and English literature too. Being required by the state to read novels, plays and poetry and make up stories out of nothing felt like a luxury that was too good to be true. I didn't know that education was supposed to be enjoyable and meant to bring out the best in us.

Returning to school following the quiet intimacy of home tutoring around the dining table was a bombardment of shouting and screaming, violence and aggression. Forced fun and frivolity mocked the crushing threat of death that surrounded me. My childish green uniform poked fun at the lethargy that clung to me. There was pushing everywhere in the corridors and I had to lay my hands over my head to protect its fragile scar. The bells announcing change of class sounded louder than an MRI scan.

My body had become a wrenched and mangled mess longing in every cell for rest. I couldn't even hold a pen properly. My brain was exhausting itself by learning new ways of navigating around the damage, forming new connections between the left and right brain. Cerebral voids, breakages, lesions and electric pathways were forcing and forging my new identity. The anti-epileptic drugs I took every day and night probably contributed to my exhaustion. Common side effects include memory problems, poor concentration, slowed thinking and movement. Every day at school, both in my mind and in every part of my body, felt like drudgery. There was only one solution.

There is an expression that was used a lot at school: *to whack it*. It means 'to play truant'. I whacked it over and over for two years.

My boyfriend, John, was far more interesting, and being with him was more educational than school. I skipped school to watch John dance in shows and perform in plays at his drama college. We travelled to Manchester on the bus discovering record shops, bookshops, quirky clothes boutiques and art galleries. I was convinced – and still am – that *whacking school* was more creative and formative than sitting in a dark landing staring at $xn + 1 = \sqrt{(17 - 5xn)}$ $x = y2$, or memorizing the periodic table.

Recovering from a brain haemorrhage as a teenager makes it difficult to separate what behaviour is normal and what is a consequence of brain and body damage. It is senseless to try to make neat separations. My parents probably found it difficult to make these differentiations too. They were exhausted and terrorized by the suffering they had seen. Fearfulness caused by what had happened and what might happen to me seemed to freeze parental authority.

Certain choices I made certainly compounded their confused anguish. My dad had a low-key party for his fortieth birthday; I was sixteen. I had been to Manchester in the afternoon and John and I both spontaneously had our noses pierced in a booth at the off-beat Corn Exchange. I walked into the living room filled with my parents' friends. My swollen nose and silver stud made quite a statement. The room went quiet; I stared at my father, smirked and padded to my room.

I decided that I would die before I was 21. I was certain that my brain would bleed uncontrollably and that would be it. Death and darkness taunted and ravaged me. Paradoxically though, fear propelled me more than it felled me. Mornings bullied me daily: death may come before nightfall so fill each second with meaning and purpose; don't die stupid or sleeping.

I counted down the days to escape school for ever. I understood full well that wishing time away contradicted my fear that I had only five years of living left, but freedom trumped time easily.

One of my most treasured memories is this:

I had just sat my final GCSE exam. I don't remember what subject it was. Other pupils were running around laughing and shrieking, taking their jumpers off to reveal their shirts so that they could sign each other's with a marker and turn the school uniform into a prized relic of the 'best years of their lives'. I turned and walked the other way, crossing the vast empty playing fields towards home. I thought to myself, beaming, 'No one can ever tell me what to do now. I'm sixteen. I'm free.'

Escape was my interpretation of freedom. I wanted to go and live abroad. I saved up by working in a chip shop after school and waitressing on Saturdays in my final year. John went to London to train as a dancer; I didn't want to go to the local College where I would be forced to be friends with people from Hollins and other people my age from different secondary schools in Accrington. There was a grammar school ten miles away but uniforms were required, which seemed perverse in every sense of the word. I felt very old.

Instead, I took part in a year abroad programme and was sent to live with a family on the outskirts of Paris. Unfortunately, there was even more algebra in the Lycée so I whacked it there too, abandoned the family and my room with a view of the Eiffel Tower, and discovered writers, artists, poets and Americans at a bookshop in the Latin Quarter on my own.

Books became my Bible. Faith had not even been packed into the attic with my school books; it had just evaporated. Novels provided new means of making sense of death. The exotic people, food and places I discovered in Paris expanded the availability of *experiences* for me to guzzle before death starved my body of breath.

French neurologists disparaged the British doctors' choice of anti-epileptic drugs I had been prescribed, and handed out a new type of pill. One afternoon, while transitioning from one drug to the other, I was standing in a carriage on the Metro on my way to Montparnasse to meet a soignée Russian who was a literature student at the Sorbonne. I sensed a molten churning in my pit; my heart rattled; twinkling lights appeared beneath the dull electric strips in the carriage. I leapt off the train at the next stop, sat next to a smoker on the bench and rested my head on my knees. The aura, whose Greek origin means breath or breeze, was blown away by the blast from the next train.

One morning I noticed that the jodhpurs I had bought from the *marché aux puces* a few months earlier didn't fit. A button popped off the Jean Paul Gaultier trousers I had found there too. The new anti-epileptic drugs were incubating fat cells via my thyroid glands. In less than two months my body ballooned beyond recognition. The skin on my thighs, stomach and legs was stretching out, struggling to contain the fresh blubber.

When I returned home months later I begged my parents to try and help me reverse my weight gain. My watching and waiting parents paid for me to see a private specialist. He asked me to undress and lie down on the trolley in the middle of the consultation room. It felt strange that he was observing my stomach and not my head. I cried as he squashed down my swollen abdomen. He offered me a new anti-epileptic drug prescription, which I accepted immediately and thankfully. The weight did not melt away, instead a grey veil of drowsiness developed.

Still convinced that death, not keys to the door, would be handed over at 21, I was convinced that I should go to university somehow so I reluctantly began to study for A levels a few miles away at the further education college in Blackburn. I walked beside St John's Church nearly every day on my way to the bus stop, passing the door to the choir vestry, but never went in. I turned away from the people I used to sing and dance with there, not in shame but – admittedly – in haughty derision. Memories of the fun of the church, especially the music, jeered at the misery that I masked from myself, as well as everyone else.

Prayer of Petition

> Out of the depths I cry to you, O LORD.
> Lord, hear my voice!
>
> Psalm 130.1–2

When a child leaves the womb, moving from darkness to light, from silence to sound, she wails. Her first breath is sounded out. For a while a child's pleasures and pains will only be expressed in wordless, incomprehensible sounds. Similarly, when we are sick the sounds our voices make may express joy, agony, sorrow, relief; it is a new lexicon of the distressed body. As we suffer we gasp, sigh, shout and cry. A body in crisis is *provoked*, that is to say, forced to give voice to experience. It is jolted out of the benign securities of the night that those who are well expect and even presume is their possession. 'I love my sleep,' say those whose sleep is safe and sound. Yet the sick body is regularly led out to endure the long, dark night. It doesn't need to be a frightening place of silence and absence though. Every utterance, every gasp, breath and movement can be directed God-ward. God neither slumbers or sleeps.

> O Lord, open thou our lips;
> And our mouths shall show forth thy praise.
>
> Morning Prayer, Book of Common Prayer

As our experience of suffering continues we sometimes begin to develop new forms of communicating our needs and discomfort. We speak differently, our voice is changed, our vocabulary is enhanced because we need to find different words for new sensations. When we find these words we are inheriting the experiences of those who have suffered before us. Also, new words for our own new pains are born that are unique to us.

Why? Help! Save me? Deliver me! Exclamations are shouted publicly to friends, fellow bedridden neighbours and doctors, though many are mouthed in private, rhetorically into the dark. Sometimes those who have never believed or been taught about a Divine Being find that their mouths declare their physical feelings and emotions to something Other and to God. Cries of pain become calls for salvation; sighs become longing for the comforting presence of God or at least something greater that is beyond themselves. Multiple unique sounds become shouts of praise, calls for truth, declarations of joy, claims to be heard and saved and sheltered. Physical distress can sometimes make atheism look like a naive fantasy.

> A crowd flowed over London Bridge, so many,
> I had not thought death had undone so many.
> Sighs, short and infrequent, were exhaled,
> And each man fixed his eyes before his feet.
>
> T. S. Eliot, *The Waste Land*

The shell-shocked sufferers commuting like ants to work at their desk jobs are silenced by their traumatic experiences of war in Eliot's epic poem of modern anxiety. They have no words to express their pain, no one to hear their cries, no place to be still in order to contemplate their experience. They are trapped and isolated silent sufferers, scared of the endless sky above them and the dark river beneath them. The instinct may be to wrestle pain down and run away from it, but recovery – both spiritual and physical – requires us to endure the night and hopefully to welcome it when it begins to become acknowledged as part of the way of recovery.

Many people who are unwell find the night very difficult. The sentimentality of *that silent night* when the baby Jesus was born beside lowing cattle, seems insulting now. Yet the hours of darkness can be a place or a time zone that, as the suffering continues or worsens and as complications arise or return, reveals itself to be rich in paradoxes and contrasts. The night can be a place of torment and refuge; hiding and revelation; despair and hope; restlessness and repose; clamour and silence; blindness and insight. Whichever way we may face and experience the night, no one can escape it.

Prayer of Preparation

The squeaks of a nurse's plastic sandals on their feet can always be heard in the night in hospital wards. The rasps of patients in the beds on the end of the ward ricochet all around. Regularly there is ordinary weary moaning, but sometimes red lights illuminate the half-dark, and a repetitive bleep calls for urgent help which is followed by the sound of a purposeful rush. In the children's hospital parents pace along corridors, perch on seats at bedsides, and pull hard on cigarettes outside. Nothing can wait till tomorrow there.

When we are ill the prospect of night no longer bears the frisson of sexual pleasure. The inevitability of the night rules out any possibility of cosy and contented rest. The long hours of night, if we are unprepared, can feel like a vast tormented vacancy. The darkness may become a bullying ogre we are scared of confronting, making us vagrants of the night. The stuffy bedroom may feel like a prison cell.

We all belong to the family of God and we are God's children: it is all right to rush to God for safety if the silence and the darkness make us feel afraid. Faith (*pistis* in Greek) may best be known as the act of trust – that is to say developing a way of being and relating in order to fall freely into God's love. It is prayer that aligns us with God, helping us to let go of control and stubbornness. In the dark long night if we are still and silent we may begin to make room for God and discover that the life of prayer, which is an inward journey, may be *lived in* as darkness falls, deepens and eventually makes way for light.

Silent Prayer

It is tempting to turn on the radio when sleep isn't easy. Being still and silent in the night can be frightening but we can learn so much about ourselves and God if we allow silence to enter in and find work in us. At first, silence can make us feel exposed, stripped and naked, but that is important. Silence may even become a refuge – but it is never an escape. Silence can liberate us, clearing away obstacles that block our hearts, purging our minds of pettiness if we can bear it for long enough.

We might presume that silence is a *thing* that is *done to us* – almost like a punishment. Silence is often stereotyped, and here in particular, it's not an order from a teacher desperately seeking calm and compliance: 'fingers on lips!' Silence, when it is created by us, in us and lived out can lead us to put our hands to our mouths in awe and wonder. That is what happened to Job when God was spectacularly revealed to him:

> Then Job answered the LORD:
> 'See, I am of small account; what shall I answer you?
>   I lay my hand on my mouth.
> I have spoken once, and I will not answer;
>   twice, but will proceed no further.'
>
> Job 40.3–5

Silence is not a commodity, although in the noisy daytime the purchase of calm through a yoga class or meditation group can feel like a luxury treat. Neither is silence an achievement, nor an experience to undergo, nor even an absence of sound, but a vast realm to be explored and adventured in. Being awake in the night in pain and unable to sleep might offer us new planes to cross when sun seems so far from the horizon.

If we resist noise, silence can break through the surface and get under our skin. At first we may notice our heart beating, reminding us that one day it will stop. And it will. If we welcome and work with silence by letting go of babble and fuss we can re-route the focus of life to the place it belongs: the heart. Our breath can be heard at last and the breath of God – the Holy Spirit – the source and quiet force of life, can be welcomed in, resuscitating the constricted soul which is trapped within the constricted and disordered body. God prays in and through our pain and discomfort. Prayer *happens* in us.

> The Spirit helps us in our weakness; for we do not know how to pray as we ought, but that very Spirit intercedes with sighs too deep for words.
>
> Romans 8.26

The first word in the Rule of St Benedict for monks and nuns is, 'Listen!' We can only hear when we are silent first; we can only speak to God because God spoke first. We will not always be silent for our true end is to praise God. Therefore, we can choose to be silent sometimes as an act of reverence. Composer John Cage's 4'33" is a piece of silent music. Its original title was *Silent Prayer*. It is a provocation to the culture of listening for the audience who have come to make meaning out of sound together. Here, they are seated – captivated by time and space in which silence is bordered. I have experienced a performance of this work and it was bizarre, shocking and moving. The audience respected unspoken rules to honour the call the composer made to be silent. Everyone was in it together.

> You called me; you cried aloud to me; you broke the barrier of my deafness.
>
> Augustine, *Confessions*, 10.27

In the silent nights the cultivation of silence gives our damaged bodies a new dignity: they are not mistakes of creations, but mysterious holy sites in which God sings songs of delight. It is important for us to respect the night, not least because our bodies' work of reparation is most effective when we are asleep.

Contemplative Prayer

It is tempting to turn on the light if we wake up in the night, sore and weary. If we stay in the dark we can discover that God can be found and *seen* in the darkness and in the unknown. The loss of dignity our bodies may have caused us to feel may make the darkness preferable. The light and the mirror reveal too much distortion and our shamed bodies shame *us* as though our bodies are not our selves anymore. The darkness may be felt as an absence, a void where nothing can be known or felt. Yet God can be revealed and known in the darkness. Within us is a divine spark waiting to be lit. Unknowing and confusion in our search for God in the night is not a sign of failure. Instead, darkness can be the place of a lack of knowing where God is revealed. So in the darkness of the night we can learn to 'un-know' rather than strain for a certainty of the presence of God through feelings, books and other well-meaning distractions. Our limitations can seem much worse in the dark. Yet God can be encountered here because God is not only known through knowledge. Wordless contemplation does not need images, but only stillness. We could see becoming ill as an invitation to be a contemplative, like Mary who sits at Jesus' feet while her sister Martha works in the kitchen. God wants us to be still and experience darkness even when it is frightening. This long night could be an invitation to lie by Christ's wounded side.

Our physical state is an advantage. We have to learn quickly when we are sick that we aren't in control. There is so much about our bodies that we don't know. We can't fix them ourselves most of the time so we have to let others try to do that for us. We are required, if we are to heal, to loosen our grasp and *let go*. The same can be said of our faith. Perhaps through our incapacity, our capacity to know God is increased. R. S. Thomas's poem articulates the frenzied attempts to experience God. But he discovers that God cannot be grasped, yet God remains.

The Absence
It is this great absence
that is like a presence, that compels
me to address it without hope
of a reply. It is a room I enter

from which someone has just
gone, the vestibule for the arrival
of one who has not yet come.
I modernise the anachronism

of my language, but he is no more here
than before. Genes and molecules
have no more power to call
him up than the incense of the Hebrews

at their altars. My equations fail
as my words do. What resource have I

other than the emptiness without him of my whole
being, a vacuum he may not abhor?

R. S. Thomas

It is tempting to get out of bed. The bedroom may feel like a
prison cell and our illness a harsh sentence. We need not go out
to find help, but go inwards. Someone went to see Abba Moses in
the desert and was told:

'Go, sit in your cell and it will teach you everything.'

Benedicta Ward, The Sayings of the Desert Fathers

It is difficult, but not impossible, for the place in which we recover
slowly, slowly, to develop into a place of contemplation. In the
dark silent room God cannot be fixed or located: God is present
in God's absence. Compass points disappear in the silent night
but there is no need for directions: God finds us. The anonymous
author of *The Cloud of Unknowing* gives a wise instruction about
the unknown presence of God dwelling within us:

Be the house and let it be the householder.

The Cloud of Unknowing, Chapter 5

Awake during the night we wait, not for the dawning of the day, nor
the presence of God, but for a still and silent breathing body being
transfigured *into* prayer, becoming a fragile embodiment of trust.

I have multiple ailments. It is very time consuming to attend to
them. *Attendre* – French: to wait. At home I have a green file for
pending hospital appointments and follow-up letters from consul-
tants. The medical history headings and current diagnoses listed at
the top in bold type grows longer with time. The collective noun
for this list is 'co-morbidities'. I travel to various London hospitals,
joining queues in outpatients clinics behind strangers whose poor
health and pains have stooped them smaller. We each clutch our
appointment letter – our lucky ticket to better health. Our illness
should unite us, but the desperation to be quickly seen and made
well separates us. Only one secretary is at the desk; she is harassed

by 10 a.m. and her greeting to me is a request for my hospital number. Stubbornly, unlike poetry, I have resisted memorizing it. The computer is slow; one man has come on the wrong day and shouts furiously at his letter; another weeps but speaks no English at all. The delay times penned on the white board behind the desk prepare us for the reality of when we really will be seen by our respective consultant in the clinic in spite of the time printed on our letters. We all slump, stifled by the stagnant heat. Firefighting pain and chaos, everyone squints as the numbers denoting overly optimistic waiting times are wiped out and projected waiting times, and the misery, lengthens, and lengthens again.

Mostly, I go alone to these appointments because getting there is tedious and being there can easily feel like time wasted. A few years ago I received a letter from a hospital telling me that I had a carcinoma on my left eyelid and was summoned to see a derma-tologist. In the letter I was encouraged to take someone with me and this encouragement scared me, as though it was preparing me for bad news about my cancer that would be easier to hear if I took someone who could absorb the horror with me.

Sickness is inconvenient. Taking responsibility for it is a job of work. Like the commitment I made when I was ordained to say daily prayer, getting help to heal my body is an act of obedience undertaken whether I like it or not, or feel anything, or remember anything. Just as I try to honour my calling as a priest, I try to honour my body. I sit silently; I try to observe; I listen to the names called before mine are repeated and repeated because the person is deaf or in the toilet; I study the delicate space between an unspeaking married couple who have travelled far in late-arriving assisted transport to be there. It can be hard to know which one is waiting for their body to be seen to. Sometimes I wait for a number to bleep which will match the one marked on my pink ticket; you know – the ones usually pulled loose at the deli counter in large supermarkets.

Prayer of Confession

The loss of control brought about by illness can be unsettling and infuriating. We want to dominate our bodies and control our thoughts. Although we cannot be masters of our bodies and minds we can be custodians of them. The edge of the conscious and unconscious mind is a threshold where mystery is more difficult to refuse entry. Our memories are described by Augustine as a storehouse and our memories are who we are; but if we have suffered trauma these memories may not be welcome. When we sleep, bizarre dreams may confound, shame and scare us. Memories return, mixed with emotions which we may feel, when awake, that we have no wish nor energy to experience all over again. They can disorientate us and our fears that arise in the night can make us feel trapped, as though our own bodies are held hostage each night. Sometimes it seems that our bodies are holding our souls and minds to ransom and only the breath is able to hold us together. Even so, the night can be long and suffocating.

Jesus offers us the gift of adoption. God is no longer the inscrutable, 'I AM', but the One to be addressed as *Abba*, the Hebrew word for Daddy, Dad, Father. God makes his home in the same way that our mother and father are the sources of our being. We know, through the life of Jesus, that we are invited to cry out to God in the night, 'Help me!' There is no need to be brave and suffer silently. Just as a mother scoops up a terrified child following a nightmare, so God makes his home in us when we cry for help. When we cry out in the night to God to be rescued we may discover that he is already there.

In the long stretched-out night, in bed, in the dark, in silence, we try to be still and unmoving. Inevitably we turn. Christ invites us to turn in our heart in repentance towards God. If we dare we can halt the chronic predictability of time by sifting through our past, recognizing in our heart and not with our eyes, that things can be different. Perhaps the seemingly endless night offers the gift of time where we are able to stare into our selves and question our authenticity.

In the parable of the prodigal son the youngest child is desperate to be independent so he leaves home. He returns home, humiliated, after making bad decisions and becoming a victim of bad luck. His father sees him on the horizon and runs to meet him with open arms. For me this is the most eloquent parable in the New Testament. God is humble and patient, watching and even expecting us to make mistakes and knowing that we need to be helped, protected and forgiven. We are free to go, free to make bad choices, and always free to return. God is forever patient and forever forgiving.

It is easy to feel alienated from the outside healthy world, not least because images and photographs of perfect sculpted bodies and straight-toothed youthful smiles are impossible to ignore. It is easy to feel estranged from our own bodies. These feelings of alienation may awaken a knowledge which resides in our hearts that home as we once knew it, is not the real end and certainly not the final destination. The shame of bad choices, self-deception and the failure that taunts us in the long dark night can be handed over to God; the yoke of regret can be lifted off our shoulders. It doesn't necessarily happen quickly though. Thomas Cranmer describes this perfectly in the General Confession in the Book of Common Prayer:

> We do earnestly repent, And are heartily sorry for these our misdoings; The remembrance of them is grievous unto us; The burden of them is intolerable.

Turning to God is a repeated act of conversion of the heart because the confession is not said once only, but daily, or at least weekly on Sundays at the Eucharist service. Paradoxically then, it seems to be the dead of night, not the light of day, that offers genuine *enlightenment*. We do not need to go anywhere for that, other than to confront whatever weighs heavily upon and within us. A gnawing sense of sin infects the body, so developing the real possibility of being liberated from regrets that dull and numb us takes time and trust. When we try and *keep trying*, our bodies begin to change; our sight brightens; we see and feel differently. We can't possess God but God can possess us; God does so by possessing our wounded body, rather than our imaginary perfect body. A sick body is not the product or evidence of sin; it is both a symbol and a means of God's grace.

If we begin to enter into the night with an open heart, hoping that God may be found in the night as well as the light, then the silent, stretched-out night might not be so oppressive. A sense of isolation where we cut ourselves off in a desperate desire for safety gives way to an internal solitude which is an interior place of our own which we do not need to flee from, but instead begin to desire to encounter more deeply. Unsurprisingly, this is everyone's life's work – for the fit as well as the suffering. Those who have endured enforced rest may have a head start here.

Prayer of the Broken Heart

At the start of liberation from dulling shame and taunts of regret that come in the night when we are recovering from illness, we may feel the gentle nudge to remain in the dark. We don't always need light to fix our loving attention on God. It is not a place we arrive at once the pain has gone. We begin to accept that God might be where the pain is. This is God's action of grace that is bitter as well as sweet. If we can begin to acknowledge that our recovery is not neat and linear we have to admit that the dawn will not make everything better. Repeatedly tracing the scars on our bodies may become a form of ritual, like praying the rosary. The marks our illness has drawn on us can become smooth and comforting lines for us to pray with. The longer we wait and the stiller we become the more we discover the deeper wordless wounds welling up from inside us. No prayer techniques will heal those quickly. There is no quick fix; there is no prayer superhighway leading us out of all this trauma. As the earth turns we can keep still in the dark. The vacuum of emptiness our illness may seem to have created can sometimes become a fruitful abyss. Sitting with this vacancy in solitude we may find more room around us to stretch out more comfortably and feel that our whole life is one of steady longing for God, rather than an endless series of experiences to enjoy one after the other.

At last, the word *courage* seems appropriate. The root of the word is *cor* – it is the Latin word for heart. This word recognizes that the seat of feelings is not the head, neither is it biceps, nor intellect, but it is the beating heart. It is here in darkness and solitude where we can become better attuned to our beating heart, as though we are hearing it for the first time.

Once we have accepted that darkness may be a place of peace and potential for the presence of the divine it may begin to feel safe to embrace the hearts beyond our own bodies. In our solitude we can move from being a victim to becoming a witness. When we do this we become active participants in the suffering world. This way, the intercession of God, who is endlessly concerned for the pain of the world, *happens in us*. Praying for the needs of others can be done and lived out through our suffering bodies. In our prayers for the suffering – for people we know who are ill, or people far away dying in war zones or famine – whether they be said alone in silence or spoken in groups and churches, we participate in the dynamic life of the Trinity by welcoming in the Holy Spirit and honouring the broken heart of Christ which is offered without condition by the Father. Our hearts are more malleable now and better able to be moulded by God's life. God's dynamic life in Trinity is not just 'up there' above the fantasy clouds, but it is also inside us, beating within our hearts.

Christ's words of consolation given to us in our suffering can be made ours in prayer for those beyond our own skin. Christ connects our suffering bodies with the suffering and pained world. His death is universal. Further, Jesus' submission to pain and powerlessness globalized the alignment of God with human suffering. The lifeblood we feel flowing within us is now co-mingled with the pain of God's entire creation.

All four Gospel writers tell of Jesus' regular retreats into solitude but it is vital to note that, for Luke, even when many people were around, Jesus would escape the crowds. The imperfect tense is used, which expresses that it was a repeated action of Jesus to act in this way.

✠

He would withdraw to deserted places and pray.

Luke 5.16

Jesus Christ, in who he is and what he does, invites silence. Jesus is the Son of the One whose identity is revealed as 'I AM WHO I AM' (Exodus 3.14). Often we see that in Jesus' obedience to the will of the Father, in powerlessness and in silence, he neither acts, reacts, nor speaks. Jesus is not only just another victim of injustice. Rather, he enters into the present moment accepting that nothing should be held back. This embodied and suffering 'I AM', who is 'of one being with the Father' as the Nicene Creed describes Jesus' divine nature, symbolizes much more than an unjust execution. Hanging there on the cross, stilled and silenced, Jesus' body speaks to us. As we try to be still before the crucifix we can learn to see his body saying something and revealing something crucial to us, which is: 'YOU ARE'. Christ confirms our existence and our connection to God who is the source of all that is good in creation. This may sound strange or even insulting for those whose bodies have never made them feel as though they are being mocked or annihilated. Yet Jesus' dead body tells us that we are more than our own death. I am because he is.

Vigil

All time belongs to God. Our earthly bodies will expire, becoming victims of what may, at first, be blindly seen as slavish, chronic time. In faith the End, including the end of our physical lives, is never truly over because all time and eternity belong to God. If we are able to enter into solitude we begin to notice that we enter into a silent dialogue with a different mode of time: *Kairos*. Here, the creativity of the present tense moment of 'now' is revealed. The silent present moment opens out the possibility of encounter with God, which may be felt as peace instead of resignation; of restfulness instead of restlessness; calm instead of terror; honesty instead of delusion.

Paul was briefly made blind following his encounter with Jesus on the road to Damascus. Perhaps the vision of Jesus was so revelatory that he needed to be sightless in order to gain insight. He had to go blind in order to see. Paul's own journey following Christ was led by conviction, not guidebooks. His instruction to the Corinthians reveals how his understanding of who Christ is and who he himself has become, is rooted in experience. 'We walk by faith,' he urges, 'not by sight' (2 Corinthians 5.7). Risk, falling and failure were possible on his every path. Yet blind faith is not our destination; instead, in the long night we pray to God and with God, not because we see, but because we cannot see.

> [Christ] departed from our sight, so that we should turn to our hearts and find him there.
>
> Augustine, *Confessions*, 4.12

Prayer of Adoration

Through our endurance of the long night our perspective might change. If we manage it, or keep trying, with our heart broken apart and our sight diminished, we learn that we do not need to charge ahead racing to the new day far away from the tedious night. We may begin to gauge our choices, not by ease or attractiveness, but by openness to the Spirit dwelling in us. We move from groping in fear through wasteful attempts at self-reliance, to stepping out fearfully in trust. Restored vision is not a question of being fixed and back to normal because if recovery means simply 'same as before' there would be no winding path towards transformation. Although doubt is understandable, complacency is the enemy of recovery. I made that mistake. Through what we do not or cannot see, we glimpse God. This is not a glib expectation: it can hurt.

The dark night transfigures our vision. We can speak Jesus' instruction, *thy will be done* with our own voice originating from our gut because now we have allowed it, lived it and seen it: the world is not ours to possess. Through the darkness, allaying our disrupting preference to put intellect before insight, we begin to see through God's prism. With our eyes in sharper focus the whole created order, including our naked bodies, begins to shout *sacred!*

When Jesus took Peter, James and John to Horeb, Jesus was transfigured. 'His face shone like the sun, and his clothes became dazzling white' (Matthew 17.2). At first the disciples are desperate to talk about what they can see as though they want to grasp and possess the experience. We need to learn to behold and be silent.

Only later should we talk, and whatever we utter shall begin in adoration and praise.

With diminished vision in a dim temple the old prayerful man Simeon sees and holds the Son that Mary dutifully places in his arms. After a long life's wait for God to restore Israel back to being God's delight, Simeon holds the infant (a word that means 'without speech'), at once receiving and offering God's gift. His prayer is charged with relief, 'my eyes have seen thy salvation'. His life can end peacefully; he sees and knows that God keeps his promises because the Messiah has come at last, just as God said. Simeon's life spent in prayerful expectation has been one of patient praise.

A renewed experience of the long, quiet, silent night after a wearisome struggle with silence, darkness and pain may change the way we greet the morning. We are expected, according to the Compline liturgy, to wait for Christ 'as the night watch looks for the morning', but the imperative to be on alert for *experience* of God when we are stuck and sore is not so easy to live up to. We may realize that our faith and our prayer no longer operates like that any more. We don't need light to see God; we don't always need speech to praise; we don't need proof to believe.

'Can you not see him waiting for you?' writes the author of *The Cloud of Unknowing* (Chapter 20), instructing his pupil about how to pray. We who are awake in the night trying to make sense of our bodies, of our faith and of our future may not easily share the author's conviction: *No*. We can't see him; we can't feel or hear him either. In the night, as we try to recover, we attempt to keep vigils in order that our lives and our bodies may become witnesses of the life of Christ and the Spirit of God settling within us.

8

Healing

Blackburn Cathedral was formerly the parish church of St Mary the Virgin. It was built in 1826 on the site of a medieval church and became a cathedral in 1926. In 1961 the gloomy Victorian windows were taken out and replaced by bright abstract stained glass and a spiky corona was placed in the lantern, or crossing as it is sometimes known, unashamedly dominating the whole interior. It is a gigantic version of the crown of nails that was fixed in my head only two years earlier, when I was 16. The first ordination of a woman priest in the cathedral took place in 2014, 20 years after women were admitted to the priesthood. I visited it briefly when I was a small child but I have still never been to a church service.

The day I sought shelter there the cathedral was shut. The thick wooden door was stubbornly ancient, in contrast to the bold 1960s windows, furniture and art inside. It was a cold afternoon and Louise had a denim jacket on. She was from London and hadn't quite adapted to the chilly damp Blackburn weather that never seemed to lift. Louise and I met at college. We spent hours in the Coach and Horses, a pub by the train station that was run by a lesbian couple, and talked about music. That evening, with my shoulders resting on the west door of Blackburn Cathedral, we kissed.

John was no longer my boyfriend, but we were still close friends. He was still studying in London and I itched to escape the north-west again, regularly catching the bus to Victoria Coach Station at weekends. John and I went to gay nightclubs such as Heaven in Charing Cross and danced till the early morning. It felt bizarre to return to A-level English class on Monday morning to read

Mansfield Park. I had discovered Jeannette Winterson, Virginia Woolf, Sappho, HD, Flaubert and Djuna Barnes. My mind was anywhere but Blackburn. One day the head of English asked me to come and see her: 'Jennie, your work is excellent. You can get an A in your exams but you have to actually come to the classes. You're missing too many classes.'

I said sorry. But I wasn't sorry. The lure of London was stronger than a single letter of the alphabet.

John had told me about a café in Soho called First Out that he thought I'd like. It was called First Out because it was the first openly gay and lesbian café in London. He took me there on a Sunday afternoon for coffee before I headed to the coach station. A female waitress with jet black hair, huge brown eyes beneath 1950s spectacles, and plummy lipstick on her small fleshy mouth took my order. We both smiled at each other. John and I sat beside the counter where she made our coffee. We went to First Out the following Sunday, and she was there again. I ordered, and made sure we sat in the same spot as the previous week, which was as close to her as we could get. I decided to stay another night so I could go to First Out alone the next day. She was working that morning. It was her coffee break. She asked, in an American accent, if she could sit at my table. I said yes.

Within two weeks of meeting Amy I quit my A levels and moved in with her in a shared flat in Brixton. My dad drove me to the coach station in Manchester and waved goodbye, bewildered and probably terrified by my obstinate desire to quit college and move to London to live with a glamorous American woman five years older than me whom he had never met. My parents knew that my desire for freedom and taste for risk were too strong to tame. They generously and graciously set me free again.

I arrived in London with a rucksack and a copy of *Oranges Are Not The Only Fruit*, by Jeanette Winterson, Accrington's most famous daughter. I threw away the anti-epileptic drugs. The fug of lethargy they induced inhibited my enthralment of London and Amy.

I got a job in a lesbian restaurant near Victoria. I took A-level classes in Hoxton, which was not trendy or arty at all then. I joined the poetry library at the Royal Festival Hall, I went to art galleries, theatres and the Prince Charles cut-price cinema in Leicester

Square. I met artists and actors from all over the world – they all worked at First Out. I watched Amy perform her one-woman show, *Gay Man Trapped in a Lesbian's Body*, at the Institute of Contemporary Art in The Mall. Amy had been in London for only two years and was infatuated by the city; we explored London and enjoyed its riches together.

I completed some A levels at last, but I had a seizure the day before my English exam. I could hardly remember my name, never mind the politics in Harold Pinter's plays and the identity of W. H. in Shakespeare's sonnets. I did not tell anyone, or ask to defer my exam. My mark, unsurprisingly, was poor.

Despite my disappointing results, I had received an unconditional place to study English at Queen Mary University of London. I was in America with Amy's family when my A-level results came out. I did not realize that you were supposed to phone the university to formally accept a place. By the time I returned to London my place had been taken.

I bought Karen Armstrong's book, *A History Of God*, in Manhattan that summer but I could not finish it. Andrew, Amy's co-worker at the café, invited us for dinner – our first London dinner party. His boyfriend, Guy, was a theology postgraduate student at King's College London and he and I talked about belief in God. I mentioned how I could not finish *A History Of God* because it infuriated me, though I couldn't put my finger on why.

'You probably know more about God than you think, Jennie,' he said.

'But I don't think I know *anything* about God,' I replied.

He smiled and handed me a book. It was Leo Tolstoy's *A Confession*.

I devoured it and it devastated me. At its heart is the necessity of faith in Christ in order to survive. 'Where there is faith there is life,' he writes, summing up his life's experience. I did not understand what faith was, nor where to go to get it. I presumed that Christianity was dead, in London at least. The parish church in Brixton, St Matthew's, seemed to have shut down. The painted sign was peeling and the huge neoclassical structure looked like a Church of England relic. There was a church on the street where Amy and I lived which had been converted into a furniture shop.

I secured a last-minute place at Goldsmiths College on the modern languages course, so four years of French and Spanish lay ahead of me. In my second year we were studying the Existentialists in my French twentieth-century literature class. These philosophers' obsession with freedom, absurdity and death compounded my encroaching despair, not least because I was almost 21. My birthday hung over me like a guillotine. I was obsessed with freedom but could not understand what to do with it – where I should channel it. Love, books and poetry did not satiate my fear of annihilation; in fact, they exacerbated it.

Early on a Sunday morning the bus dropped me off at Southwark Cathedral, but it was closed; another door shut. I didn't turn back though; the first service would be in 20 minutes so I walked along the Thames, letting the wind and the rain wake me up.

Holy Communion was in a side chapel. I didn't care what the service was, I just needed to be in a church, one where no one would ask me anything. There was a handful of people there; it was dark. I sat at the back; the priest was very old. My stare switched between the tiled floor, the candles, the altar, the priest's serene face and his hands lifted in supplication. My breath was steady but my stomach churned. It felt as though I was at once observing and participating in an ancient, faintly familiar solemn drama.

Standing, my eyes were fixed on the chalice and the host that the priest was lifting up as he said, 'Draw near with faith. Receive the body of our Lord Jesus Christ which he gave for you and his blood which he shed for you. Eat and drink in remembrance that he died for you and feed on him in your hearts by faith with thanksgiving.'

And so I did.

Blood and Water

By the mingling of this water and this wine
may we come to share in the mystery of Christ
who humbled himself to share in our humanity.

Priests' private prayer at the Eucharist

Water is poured from crystal cruets; sweet wine flows into ancient silver chalices as the priest prepares the elements of bread and wine that will become the focus of the Eucharist service. Among the embroidered linen and surrounded by vibrant silks a celebrant is safely housed by a chasuble while the gory horror of Jesus' crucifixion is remembered. In Jesus, the Word made flesh, God has created intimate and physical relations with us through his human experience. A flagellated back, nailed hands, and a knifed waist from which blood and water flowed is God's chief and most eloquent communication. God acts, reveals and speaks in the torture of his Son's sacrificial suffering. Spilt blood becomes a cup of blessing; flowing blood is the Church's life force.

'This is my body given for you.'

'This is my blood shed for you.'

Each person who holds out their hands, whether in a prison, chapel royal, mountain top or hospice, is reached by God and becomes holy ground. We offer our own longing in our cupped hands as we wait for the priest to draw near. In this moment there is a tenderly heartbreaking action of giving and receiving. But still, among the purity of symbol and the nobility of tradition, the chaos and mess of human life remains. Symbols are subverted for us through the wounds, blood, sweat and tears of Christ.

Spilt Blood

Neat hospital corners create taut sheaths of bleached white sheets. Those preparing them fight daily defilement. They lose every time. Bodies leak, ooze, drip, fester, cut, seep, weep, gape, sag. Soil – the earth – from which all life grows is the shaming act committed by a person who has lost mastery of his own body. All births – *including Jesus'* – begin in a nest of blood and watery amniotic fluid which, when the fruit is ripe, is disgorged from a woman's womb. It is life force, a prerequisite for life, not a shameful spillage. Yet it seems to be that every drop of fluid we allow to fall drains us of dignity. We cannot clamp our bodies shut. The art of an embalmer is to conceal and restrain the life that flows out of a dead body. A refrigerated coffin continues to create the comforting illusion that our bodies, even in death, can contain themselves. Whoever said that cleanliness is next to Godliness?

Wash me, and I shall be whiter than snow.

Psalm 51.7

Sometimes it can feel as though our bodies are warring violently in us, turning every inch into a war zone. Breath and a beating heart pumping blood can sound strangely triumphant as it marks time like a troop resisting defeat and chaos. Multiple parts of our bodies seem to fight between themselves and we just have to wait, unable to negotiate peace on our own. Drugs jostle for might, and rest must wrestle for calm. Our bodies may not seem our own any more: somewhere our 'selves' – that essential part of us located somewhere in relation to the symbolic heart and the mysterious brain – are in exile, trapped within this foreign hostile land we once thought was our own private colony. The pain increases: our sick bodies are disgracing us, our bodies now made weak by illness become signs of punishment. Barrages of 'serves you rights', 'told you so's' and 'oh dears' sound like torture. We ask ourselves, God and others, *What have I done wrong? Who will lead me home? Who will rescue me? How long will this occupation last?* The seeping, stinking body may look and feel repugnant. But this is the reality, and we cannot find flight somewhere cleaner, safer, bloodless because there is no life, nor true freedom there. To be healed or to be holy is not an act of being made clean. Although it is holy oil that is daubed on our forehead at our baptism its symbolizes that we are marked by blood and not bleach. Blood that was once a curse has become a blessing.

For I desire steadfast love and not sacrifice.

Hosea 6.6

Flow of Blood

Blood is a sign of life as well as death. Yet the viscous flow of blood in both animals and people is often presumed to be defiling, a shameful sign of pollution, a sickly cocktail brew of our own making. Blood is contradictory: we need it, we loathe it. The purity codes in the book of Leviticus lay out strict rules so that blood and bodily fluids cannot contaminate the human body and therefore restrict our connection to God.

> I have said to the people of Israel: You shall not eat the blood of any creature, for the life of every creature is its blood; whoever eats it shall be cut off.
>
> Leviticus 17.14

In the Jewish tradition food from animals is drained of blood, whereas the act of sacrifice through the spilling of blood is an expiation of guilt. The gruesome ritual of animal sacrifice was cathartic and helped the people of Israel to ritually understand themselves and their frustrating and complex relationship with God. Spilt blood was enacted in order to try to restore a broken covenant. Blood is also a sign of salvation. At the escape from captivity in Egypt, God gave his people clear instructions to each household:

✠

> When I see the blood, I will pass over you and no plague shall destroy you.
>
> Exodus 12.13

Unfortunately the close alignment of purity with God has not disappeared. Perhaps we cannot convince ourselves that our flesh is sacred and even our guts are graced. Jesus' arrest, torture and crucifixion have been ritualized in the Stations of the Cross. In this liturgy we follow Jesus' Way to his death in measured steps: Jesus is stripped naked, whipped, falls to the ground, falls again, and a third time, sweats, bleeds and covered in Roman saliva. In one of the stations that has entered into the tradition of marking Jesus' steps towards death we meet Veronica wiping the perspiring face of Jesus in a tender act of compassion. The garment reveals an image of Jesus' face. It is a *vera nica* – a true image (in Latin) in blood of the suffering man she loved. A garment is defiled by a criminal's blood which later becomes a sacred relic. Blood, sweat, tears and rough gashes on the skin of Jesus create paradoxes that must be faced by us in order for healing to bear fruit. The disciple Thomas touched the wound in Jesus' side and it was Christ's open flesh that gave birth to the disciple's trust in his promises that his life meant much more than what could be seen and touched in the flesh.

'Reach out your hand and put it in my side . . .' Thomas answered him, 'My Lord and my God!'

John 20.27–28

Stemmed Blood

Immediately her haemorrhage stopped.

Luke 8.44

There is an unnamed woman who appears in Matthew, Mark and Luke's Gospels. Her polluting flow of menstrual blood excludes her from work, her community and from worship in the synagogue. No one can find a cure; she was probably dying as Luke writes that her flow of blood was getting worse. As a Jew she was born under the covenant and was subject to it. She was therefore defined by defilement. Eradicating bloody stains from sheets and clothes would have been her main activity for 12 years. She had 'heard about Jesus'. Brave as well as desperate, when Jesus is walking the woman breaks through the surrounding crowd and stretches out to touch him. Jesus is embraced by a bleeding woman. Her touch does not defile Jesus at all. In fact, it releases God's glory that dwells in him. The flow of blood stops; she is restored. 'Go in peace,' Jesus tells her; she can now participate in worship, and community life. She is not cleaned up; she is set free.

The woman's healing does not end when the blood dries up. Jesus calls her 'daughter' – she is a new disciple, a member of Jesus' household, which is not restricted by purity or blood ties. Although she was despised because of her body the woman knows in her body that she is better. In that instant when Jesus and she touch, God's new kingdom – a territory co-created by Jesus and those attracted to him – expands. God is always creative.

> This is the one who came by water and blood, Jesus Christ, not with the water only but with the water and the blood.
>
> 1 John 5.6

Jesus not only makes a new Way to God, but also a new world order which is perhaps seen most clearly and most comfortingly when he heals those who are sick. An epileptic boy is released of a malignant trauma and shame; an ostracized leper is cleansed; a dying pubescent girl survives; a Roman soldier's servant lives; the sick are healed on the Sabbath. Taboos are shattered, power structures are broken, religious certainty is tested, the overlooked are spotted, the crazed are forgiven, the powerful humiliated, the shamed are gracefully honoured, the exhausted are refreshed, the disgusting are touched with tenderness, new communities are forged. Previously locked-down networks are ruptured, opening up new possibilities of reconciliation and liberation between people and God. Sometimes revelation has to be searched for in unsightly places.

✠

Our own healing story will not be recorded by evangelists, nor will it be so dramatic, immediate or as obvious as those sick people Jesus met, but each healing body is a living epiphany where God is made manifest. Unlike the post-Christmas epiphanies we mark in January, there are no camels bearing witness to the marvel of our survival, no brave prophet like John the Baptist making way for us as we shuffle out of the hospital. We have to make meaning out of our healing, and make a place for God in it. Recovery offers new and fresh ways of seeing and being alive, if we are able to make connections between our own private experience and the world beyond our bodies. Christ's healing up of wounds breaks open a new way of living. Belief offers the hope, the expectation even, that the divine initiative of God which is revealed and released in Jesus has not waned. The challenge of faith is to learn and relearn to live with, to believe in, and to marvel at God's tireless breaking in to the mess of life even when it may not look pretty. As the Angle Gabriel said to Mary,

'Nothing will be impossible with God.'

Luke 1.37

Christ attracts people to see differently. Sin, an unfashionable and abused word, can sometimes be defined as the resistance to change and an inability to see differently. Eyes closed shut may not be signs of holiness, but of ignorance. Christ calls for the transfiguration of our vision. Although dramatic cure is a fantasy, our healing – slow and frustrating as it may be – is not as mundane as 'back to work' at all. Beginning to heal well gives us the opportunity to become visionaries.

'I believe; help my unbelief!'

Mark 9.24

Sealed Blood

Miracles make some of us nervous: did they happen *then*? Do they happen *now*? When a child is close to death most people – whether they profess a faith or not – long for a miracle to happen. If the child recovers, has a miracle occurred? If we are hoping to recover and trying to understand what has happened to us, and even question if there is a purpose to our illness, then reading and thinking about the healing miracles can help us to frame the right questions and offer new ways of thinking about what healing might actually look and feel like for us. The healing miracles in the New Testament are never ends in themselves. Jesus does not just 'fix' things. We need to learn that our illness and our recovery – however slow or partial it may feel – are not ends in themselves either. Illness is not a blip that will be best forgotten when the pain has receded. We may begin to recognize, thanks to the gift of Christ, that there is more to us than flesh and blood.

> He heals the broken-hearted,
>   and binds up their wounds.
>
> Psalm 147.3

If we can link God and the healing miracles of Christ to our own recovery, however slow or partial, Jesus expands both our understanding of God and ourselves. We may even begin to allow the two to enmesh into our recovering body. Jesus is not a magician, nor an exorcist, nor a charismatic showman. Rather, Jesus is revealed as the divine Messiah, the anointed one, chosen by God to transform and anoint by healing in return. Through his work with the sick, God's glory is revealed in and through the sick and disturbed people Jesus serves. This may sound strange to those who prefer to think of Jesus as nice, and Christianity tame and polite. Jesus is at ease with his power as if it flows through his bloodstream. God's cosmic creation of every particle that exists and Jesus' intimate creative acts of healing are entirely compatible. It is interesting that many of Jesus' healing miracles took place in private. It is as though Jesus could not stop himself from healing; it was central to his nature. He didn't heal in order to prove anything, only to reveal God's love. Jesus' touch contaminated people with it.

At times when we are uncertain about God's place in our understanding of what is happening to our bodies, the classic assertion that science answers 'how' the world is, and God answers 'why' the world is can be helpful, but this is by no means neat and tidy. There are limits in our understanding of how the world works, and much of it remains a mystery. And that is *good*. Similarly, there are only limited answers to why the world is as it is. Faith does not require certainty, but faith certainly requires curiosity in order to trust that God *is* and God *knows*. I am not ashamed of the healing miracles in the Bible although I don't find them easy to explain. They are just there, revealing more about God to us. I believe that the Word was made flesh; I believe that flesh and blood that is maimed or restored is created and upheld by the Maker. And the Maker has new names: the Messiah, the Way, Friend, the Lamb: Love.

✠

The scar on my head is quite smooth. The surgeon cut it open in exactly the same place the second time. I imagine him remembering me with his scalpel in his hand, angry at himself either for having too much faith in my strength, or too much confidence in his handiwork when he stopped the flow of blood from the burst artery four years earlier. I could not wash my hair for weeks following surgery. I could smell the blood, iron rich, that was unable to be masked by antiseptic fluid. The smell pervaded my hospital bed and my memory has lodged it. When I am reading alone I often stroke the sealed wound; it is straight and smooth. Am I being comforted by it, protecting it with my hand, or is it a memento mori?

My sister said it was a terrifying shock to see so much of my hair shaven off and to be confronted by blood caked and stained around my head. The sewn-up head helped her acknowledge that something had happened inside my skull. The scar and the shorn scalp reassured her that something had been fixed. But a healing wound does not necessarily denote a safe and healed body. Recovery can be deceptive and difficult to measure. The government Department for Work and Pensions may create questionnaires for ill people, but petty tick-box questions mock the nuances, the slowness and the complexities of the healing journey.

Each wound is an encrypted story, and every scar is pain enfleshed in a fused line. It is like braille carved out for the finger to learn, read and remember. For some, a scar may be a trophy telling a story of triumph. For one, an uncoverable scar may be a living sign of humiliating defeat. Scars can be signposts that only point backwards: a wrong turn. A scar may mark a line crossed, or a transgression. Some scars are touchstones of survival.

Some wounds are hard to let heal; the urge to open them can give a thrill of relief and a whiff of independence. For others there is no wound to observe smoothing itself out because the illness is invisible. Unexpectedly, these invisible wounds can be poked and bleed, but it is felt in the gut, in the heart, the brain and on the cheeks where unwelcome tears flow.

Our wounds brand us, they are hieroglyphics that Christ's wounded body may help decipher. Grafted skin can be seen as Christ's grafted on to us, rehousing our sore human flesh. A scar – *any scar* – can be a call to prayer.

Our scars and sores can help us understand our healing and our bodies. A closed wound is not a finishing line. Our scars might be used to read our own selves better. As we read them, we learn to make faith in Christ's wounds the grammar required for us to create some sort of understanding of how our wounds connect with Christ's body, especially his wounds. We can connect and conjugate our scars, not only into Christ's wounds, but also in the healed wounds of those people who were physically graced by the touch of Christ in the healing stories in the Gospels. Grammar is not easy for most of us at first, and it can be dull and boring, but expressing ideas and naming objects is impossible without it. The grammar we need here in order to make sense of our healing scars has no rule book, but is not so easy to learn, nor is it so obvious. We need people to learn it with us. There are some stumbling blocks and quirks to reading meaning into our healing scars. But the key rule is that the grammar is always Christ the Word made flesh and its logic is his crucified body.

It is easy to cover up our wounds and never even begin to interpret the work and life of God in and on our bodies. The naked flesh of Jesus, fresh and wet with his mother's own fluids, and the naked flesh on the cross might be an affront to us if we are desperate to put on our old clothes again and get straight back to work. If our scars are still painful and the wounds still open, we should use them to read our bodies differently. The delicacy of seeping wounds can help us respect what has happened to us.

The Paradox of Blood

Interpreting our open wounds through the open wounds on Christ's wrists and the healing of the bleeding woman may help us to heal better, but not necessarily quicker. We must learn to live with the paradoxes that our interpreting work may reveal. A wound may be read as a shaming sign of lost potency, but in accepting limitations we can discover an altogether new sort of strength. An open wound might first be read as a chink in our armour, yet that chink is a symbol of God's active participation in our recovery. The wound does not have to be a silent void.

God is Trinity, not an abstract deity reigning petulantly above us. God *is* perpetual movement – three persons, Father, Son and Spirit acting in one divine nature. God does not restrict this movement to himself alone. Instead, God is poured out upon us. The wounds we are desperate to heal and efface from our bodies and our memories could become for us a sign of God's sharing of himself *within us*. The Holy Spirit – the outward activity of God – works through us and in us, not on the surface.

We have been given the gift of freedom but we can sometimes take our own bodies hostage. If we let ourselves go, especially through resisting control, we can let God speak in us and we can begin to participate in the life of God, in God's divine dance. Dancing might not come naturally, nor even be possible for a time. We can invite God to ingratiate himself in our wounds and be given new words, new ways of expressing how the world looks now with transfigured vision and a changed body. We have to create our own way of expressing what we see and feel, remembering that – hard though it may be to grasp – the grammar holding it together is the wounded Word made flesh.

✠

Speak, LORD, for your servant is listening.

1 Samuel 3.9

Jesus washed his disciples' feet during a meal. Shortly afterwards his friends would use those feet touched by the hands of the Son of God to run away from him. They were unable to connect Jesus' desire to kneel and clean their feet as a humble servant with his humiliation on the cross.

The Paradox of Grace

God's grace is not always easy to connect to our own experience, perhaps because we seem to think that we have to earn God's goodness. Jesus knew he would be betrayed by those he depended on to carry out God's wish. It did not stop him loving them. The sick people he healed were not saints, but their physical and mental needs revealed Jesus' divinity. Their bodies' *faults* unsheathed their faith; their recovery exposed the judgements of society; their hope highlighted the narrow vision of the fit and well. The healing miracles are miniature revelations of the counter-intuitive rule of God which so often appears too good to be true. Yet with each gift of healing, those who were there and those who encounter the stories of Jesus' miracles through the Bible, or in churches, are taught to try and see things differently. The grace of God has to be graciously received in order that new birth, new eyes and new hearts be made. The gentle rule of God's kingdom is unbounded, but we have a choice to let ourselves be part of it.

No one deserves to be sick and no one deserves to be healed. Deserving is a word that should be banned from Christianity. God's ways are still not our ways, but we are all – at best – striving to learn what 'thy will be done' means uniquely to each of us with every new day. So much of God's loving activity goes unnoticed. We owe God nothing; God needs nothing from us. The glory of God is ours to discern and behold; it is a gift given to lift our hearts. God does not need to do this; God *is this*.

It is God's grace that comes first, not our list of requirements to help make life bearable, decent, fun. There is no citizenship test to be part of God's kingdom, but there is a culture which has to be learned and subsequently *incorporated*; that is to say, imbibed and embodied by us. Our bodies must learn humility. Mostly this involves waiting. The nature of sin is not always grounded in the monstrous heinous dramas. Sin starts more simply, more insidiously, by turning away from the love of God and creating idols for ourselves: pride.

Scars can take a long time to heal. Closed scars can create illusions of progress and perfection. It is tempting to turn away from God in order to rush ahead on our own straight superhighway towards a fantasy version of normality and strength. Dramas make the heart beat faster, future-facing ignores the unfinished things from yesterday and the boring tasks of today. Instead, it might be better to dare to sit, daring to face our nakedness and, like the psalmists and the prophets, name the wounds and the scars which tell our stories and redescribe pain. We cannot control the flow of blood, the doubling of cells. Stripping ourselves of certainty and self-ownership may be the most healing act we can offer to ourselves, and may be the most gracious act of worship to God we can perform. Our bodies have the potential to become living sacraments.

The Paradox of Symbols

The bodies of those Jesus healed were not only made well, they remain symbols for us of the new relationship God was inaugurating through Jesus. Today their lives and bodies are teachers and reminders of a renewed way of being ill and being in relationship with God, and with each other. We have to keep interpreting these signs, not least because Jesus upends what was once fixed, safe and clear. The pollution of blood is now written into the new narrative of God; a viscous, caking, defiling bodily fluid becomes a holy living sacrament. We are not determined by purity. The woman's debilitating and humiliating flow of blood is stopped; Jesus, the One without sin, is wounded and blood flows freely from his naked body. This is God with us. Polluting blood is offered now as a means of a new relationship with God which we call covenant. This new covenant is an offering of friendship. There are no laws, though we impose them because we are unable to believe in the plenitude of God's self-emptying grace shown beautifully and gruesomely in the crucified Christ. The crucifixion is the ultimate sacrifice, not to assuage an angry deity, but to set us free from self-hatred, self-destruction and self-obsession. The wounded body of Jesus is offered as a just-about-breathing body for us to aspire to. Our wounds, not our politeness, can form us into his likeness.

By his wounds you have been healed.

1 Peter 2.24

Defiling bodily fluids became a cup of life, a holy fruit. The blood that was daubed on the lintels of the Israelites' doors in order to deliver them from slavery is spilt out of Christ's torn and disfigured body. Therefore, we can be healed by the sight and the belief in the horror that God chose to embody. Our hands clasp Christ's flesh: it is a new manna, and our lips are dipped in sweet blood which trickles into our bloodstream. There is no quick fix, but this is a living and healing offering for us to take to our lips and drink.

9

Hope

It was about after midnight. I was dancing when I spotted Guy at the other side of the room at the well-known gay nightclub, Duckie, at the Royal Vauxhall Tavern. Saturday nights are Duckie nights, a weekly club co-founded by Amy and her friend Simon. The DJs spin a variety of tunes, but Duckie's holy trinity is David Bowie, Morrissey and Kate Bush. Cabaret artists from octogenarian Yodellers to cutting-edge contemporary dancers perform on stage. It is an eclectic nightspot for the intelligent LGBT+ crowd. When I finished my late shift selling CDs in the Rock and Pop department of Virgin Megastore on Oxford Street I sometimes worked on the door, taking the admission fee and stamping hands with *DUCKIE!* as proof of payment.

I approached Guy and shouted in his ear, 'I've been to church!' He smiled and shouted back, 'Do you want to come to *my* church?' I nodded, still dancing.

'I'll pick you up tomorrow morning at 10.'

Guy pipped his horn outside our flat in Brixton; we crossed Lambeth Bridge and drove to a quiet street round the corner from Westminster Abbey. The hushed church we stepped into was small and smelt exotic. I followed Guy, sat beside him and stared at the lavish gilt interior. An organ was playing a restrained tune which I now recognize as Satie's *Gymnopédies*. The air was reverent, but relaxed and gentle. The vicar smiled a welcome and nodded serenely to Guy.

Men in white robes entered, carrying candles, a cross and a silver box on chains which was swung, chugging sweet smoke. The small congregation made signs of the cross; bells were rung at particular moments; words were sung in a foreign language; solemn silence was created; heads bowed in prayer and lifted up when the chalice was raised; the sermon was short and had poetry in it.

My body absorbed every sensory act of the Eucharist service. I had stepped into an unknown place and yet I felt found there; I was both at home and afar from myself. The carefully shaped and structured hour of lavish austerity held my body and my mind still.

There was *real* coffee afterwards, and wine too. Young people and a few elderly women gathered, unhurried and charming. Everyone seemed to joke and smile warmly and playfully. The vicar introduced himself and poured me a glass of wine.

'Would it be possible to go with you next week?' I asked Guy on our way home.

'Of course,' he replied. 'Same time next week.'

On our subsequent journeys home Guy tried to answer my endless questions such as: 'What does "Christ will come again" mean?' 'What does *Kyrie Eleison* mean?' 'Why is Jesus the lamb of God?' 'What is the Word made flesh?' 'Why make the sign of the cross?' Sometimes we both held out hands at the altar rail inked with the Duckie! stamp fresh from the night before. I arrived home from church transfigured by the beauty, mystery and intelligence of it all.

When I began to go to St Matthew's Westminster alone I would arrive very early, sit still, stare at the golden Arts and Crafts triptych on the east wall behind the altar and at the tabernacle housing the body of Christ. I'd wonder and wander in my head, readying myself for what might happen to me in the service. I always took a handkerchief. It was a process of letting go. I was 21 and I had not yet died. An unfamiliar peace settled in me, stilling me, smoothing out the jagged terror of freedom and holding steady the torturing absurdity of death and life.

✠

Someone told me that there were convents where you could stay to be silent and pray for a few days. They said it might be a good idea for me to go on a retreat. It was a new word for me, a new and exciting concept.

Sister Evelyn at the Convent of St Mary the Virgin, Wantage, in Oxfordshire, welcomed me, showed me my sparse single room and pointed out the prayer times. I spent four days there, mostly in silence, but met Sister Evelyn each morning for an hour of hushed discussion. She soon realized that I knew virtually nothing about the Gospels or the liturgy, but she was gentle and perhaps bemused by my presence there in the austere Anglican convent. I attended every service in the day and evening, mouthing the endless round of psalms and observed every bow. I spent times of silence in the chapel crying tears of confusion, ecstasy and relief. When I walked away from the convent guest house to return to London the bell was ringing, calling the nuns to prayer. I prayed in my heart, silently announcing that I was ready to offer my body and my life to God in an endless stream of praise.

I wanted, *needed*, to offer thanks for being alive. The compulsion of thanksgiving and worship to God was rooted not only in my mind, but in my body too. I believed that my body should be an offering of thanksgiving, as though it belonged better in the sanctuary of a church, pouring itself out, prostrated, where my breath and blood could be offered in a life of sacrifice, giving back to God what God had given me, in a mutually endless flow.

I bought a Bible, a book of Daily Prayer and John Macquarrie's classic hefty tome, *Principles in Christian Theology*, which Guy recommended. I took these and a copy of *The Rattle Bag*, a poetry anthology edited by Ted Hughes and Seamus Heaney, with me to Havana, Cuba, where I spent six months studying Spanish as part of my degree. I explored the churches all over the city, prayed daily, worked through the theology book and dipped into poetry. My imagination, my soul and my intellect was struck and unleashed there.

When I returned to London I declared to Amy that I felt I should become a priest. It was a strange but not unexpected announcement, and one that was easier to accept than my whispered musings months earlier that I might enter a convent for life. She understood my intentions to be ordained even though she knew that it was not going to be easy. Amy was raised in a Protestant Christian family in New Jersey, but no longer went to church. She was supportive and later joined St Matthew's Westminster too. It was clear to her that my renewed faith was tempering some of my existential anxieties and fear of death. I am told that I was a little bit easier to live with.

There are probably few people who explore their vocation to the priesthood before their faith has been confirmed by a bishop. My vicar and I agreed that I should be confirmed as soon as possible, so I knelt before the Bishop of London, Richard Chartres, with the children from St Matthew's primary school on an ordinary Tuesday afternoon. Two years later I would sit across from him in his seventeenth-century home in the shadow of St Paul's Cathedral attempting to articulate why he should trust me and anoint my head with oil, sealing my offering as a servant of God; a priest in the Church of England.

When my language degree was almost complete I was interviewed by the eminent theologian Colin Gunton for a place on the Post Graduate Diploma in Theology at King's College London. I was accepted on the full-time one-year course and I helped fund it by working as a housekeeper for David Blunkett. On my first day in his Cabinet Minister official residence in Belgravia I knocked over and smashed the kettle, on the second day I broke the vacuum cleaner, and on the third I phoned a friend to find out how to iron a shirt. I did not disclose to David Blunkett that I was half blind and epileptic, nor did I admit that I had never changed a hoover bag, nor scrubbed a floor. The apartment was huge and I did most of my theology study on his dining table. I took a course in Christology, another in the doctrine of creation and another in the Gospels. I wrote my dissertation on the fifth-century Cappadocian doctrine of the divine and human natures of Jesus. With a PgDip under my belt I became a pastoral assistant at St Matthew's Westminster under the tutelage of Father Philip Chester. I learned about intercessions, preached, prayed and visited parishioners while the Church of England decided whether or not they agreed with my desire to be ordained as a deacon and priest.

Going through the Byzantine process of discernment towards ordination to the priesthood was bewildering and slow. Each time I was asked to give an account of my sense of vocation the starting point was always my brain haemorrhage. Carefully covering up my relationship with Amy seemed more pressing than disclosing key facts about my poor health and co-morbidities. Neither my blindness nor my epilepsy was ever discussed. I was still not taking anti-epileptic drugs although I did have seizures sporadically. I had a seizure in Cuba, in New Jersey, and one on the morning of my final French exam at Goldsmiths. I also had a seizure in a tutor's office in Westcott House in Cambridge, a theological college where I was spending the night with a view to training for the priesthood there and to be interviewed for a place. The office had a small bed in it which was my room for the night. When the pre-seizure aura burst out I did not call for help – there was no one there anyway. The following morning I was still trapped in the brain-scrambled, post-fit fog when I met the academic tutor with a sore head and a bloody lip that I must have bit during the seizure. I am still amazed that, not only was I accepted, but was also offered to take the Cambridge University Tripos as part of my training for the priesthood.

Light in the Darkness

Scientists spend fine summer days inside windowless laboratories frowning faithfully into microscopes. Staring into black and white screens without lights, neurologists assess electronic images of brains whose circuits have faulty breaks, gaps or growths. Operating theatres, spotlit and strip-lit, are filled with congregations of well-groomed men and women in white coats and blue scrubs peering beyond a body's skull, taking turns to inspect the brain's mysterious dark jelly core through the microscopic camera.

Medical science is rooted in hope so it's fair to say that the human body is the epicentre and embodiment of hope. Research is the act of finding light in the darkness, of eradicating chaos and resisting destruction. Prone and heavily anaesthetized, the blacked-out sick patient is only covered in a light backless cloth, easily untied and unsheathed with one swift lift of the arm. The only other garments covering the body are white paper pants and thick tights with big holes for big toes to help veins circulate blood safely. Both the fragile body and the tireless explorers of it hope for revelation. For a scientist every day holds the potential for further enlightenment.

Our bodies are gifted by God; they are affirmed by Jesus the incarnate Word; they are enlivened by the Holy Spirit. Yet below the fragile film of skin there are so many dark places: the rivulets of blood, the snaking long intestine, the spongy marrow in the spine. The flesh, blood and bone that forms us is a mystery to ourselves with a drive of its own. However much we honour our bodies we must let them be, and hope that the heart doesn't forget how to beat.

We can easily forget who we are if we begin to feel a sense of hopelessness about our bodies. Hopelessness can be a *thing* or dreaded lurking feeling that creates a dark and narrow future for us. Our personal stories, our past, our longings that got us to this place seem to vanish. A malignant form of darkness takes over: despair. This place of despair is not an environment where the imagination can thrive in order to help us see what the future might look like. The past, the present and the future are without form when we are hopeless, and days which are dominated by death and decay have no shape or pattern. We become no-body. Any notion of grace from God, which may once have been felt and treasured, seems absurd, even insulting. God sounds too good, and prayer wasteful. The inevitability of decay seems over-whelming for those whose illness has forged an absence of hope which in the psalms is often described as a 'pit'.

Certainly, despair is to be expected at times; it may even be required at some stage in everyone's life. To fear is to be human, but our vocation is to not let it dominate and obscure God. When our despair seems to have reached its most intense we can take in the darkness and begin to live alongside it, rather than ignore it and banish it like a school bully at the door or a mad dog. *Despair and fear is here and it is real.* Our whole sick body may become a *land of deep darkness.* It is an unfamiliar, hostile, alien land. We can get lost within our own bodies that seem to have been made strange by pain and the intrusion of professional strangers. We may in time begin to long for light, but we need to take in the darkness first. This requires honesty because at some point it becomes necessary to admit to ourselves and to others that we need help and want change. If we accept that we are lost and confused we may allow ourselves to be found, or at least discover where to turn in order to discover where light may shine. Our bodies will never be as they once were, but it is in living in the fearsome darkness where we can begin to dare to long – and then yearn – for change. This is the essence of hope.

> I waited patiently for the LORD;
>> he inclined to me and heard my cry.
> He drew me up from the desolate pit.
>
> Psalm 40.1–2

Seasons of Darkness and Light

> 'He will come to save you.'
> Then the eyes of the blind shall be opened,
> and the ears of the deaf unstopped;
> then the lame shall leap like a deer.
>
> Isaiah 35.4–6

Advent

The season of Advent begins as the darkness deepens into winter. We begin to long for light and hope that relief will be found, or even find us. Advent is a metaphor for waiting for something better to come that will improve our existence. We are reminded in this season that the Old Testament prophets point the way to true light. Their lyrical voices cry out that things can and will one day be different. These are not just historical documents or ancient poetry: these persistent prophets point to our bodies, urging us to believe that our bodies may be imagined as a new Israel – a new kingdom which God longs to rescue and love. Having hope that our health may improve does not require us to make predictions about exactly what God will do to us. Our greatest and most risky hope is that God is the One who keeps God's promises. Our attempt to be patient in our longing to be found and loved align us with every person in the Bible who longs for relief. The prophets whisper their encouragement in our ears. Now though, the voice is Christ's, and the breath is God's Spirit. We can also be part of the story of the fulfilments of his promises, rather than spectators or passive, sleepy readers. Our recovering bodies and our stories will also become signs of God's divine work.

> What has come into being in him was life, and the life was the light of all people. The light shines in the darkness, and the darkness did not overcome it.
>
> John 1.3-5

Nothing at all is hidden from God. Light, which was created out of nothing by God, cannot ever be completely dimmed. This is the core of our faith and it is not a concept: it is embodied in Jesus. A fresh way of participating in the life of God is opened up to us. *Something new and important that was always promised has really happened!* This is perhaps the best way to interpret the meaning of *Euangelion*, which we know in English as 'gospel'. The promised hope is revealed in this man – Jesus. Listen to him; watch and be convinced in your heart as well as your mind that this news relates to you as well.

Christmas

> And we have seen his glory.
>
> John 1.14

The light of Christ banishes deception. What is hidden or forgotten is revealed to us. There is no need to seek truth frantically far beyond ourselves. There are fewer shadows if we put ourselves in Christ's light. We cannot deceive ourselves so easily here. Light is not a means of purification; it makes way for truth. Telling the truth of our selves begins by putting ourselves – naked – in the light of Christ. We know now, following the experience of illness and pain and despair, that the quest to discover *who* we are, not *what* we are is Jesus' challenge to us. If we step into the light offered by God we may be able to refamiliarize ourselves with our bodies as though we are being led to a home which is both familiar and new. The Bible ends with a vision of glorious light and beauty that is transformed through Christ's birth, his death and his resurrection:

> The holy city Jerusalem . . . has the glory of God and a radiance like a very rare jewel, like jasper, clear as crystal.
>
> Revelation 21.10–11

The humility of the Nativity is crucial for us as we learn to let light in. The birth of Christ was dangerous and hidden; its circumstances were ludicrous. A statusless child is born in a shed during the night. Perhaps this is the whole point of it for those of us who feel desperate in our hope that something good, something better may come out of this dark, wretched time of illness. Bizarre circumstances do not exclude the will and work of God.

Holy ground is no longer 'out there'. The sacred is enfleshed and every ligament, every object bears potential for moments of becoming graced by eternity. It can become very easy to expect very little. Our bodies can feel like a formless void, a sludge of matter without prospect of being shaped. But it is important to remember that it is a void which opens the Bible in the book of Genesis:

> The earth was a formless void and darkness covered the deep.
>
> Genesis 1.2

We might see the entire sweep of the Bible as the narrative of our body's journey, with its secret beginning, its mythic tales, historic chronicles, childhood tales, adolescent misdemeanours, learning of the law and wisdom, getting lost, becoming sick, being found and healed and changed.

We need vision, bravery and imagination to confront our bodies as they are: imperfect *and* glorious. We have to keep learning this because it sounds crazy. The violent deformity was inflicted upon Christ by a humanity which prefers the stable comfort of darkness to the precarious potential of light. Beauty and perfection have been recalibrated now because of Christ's birth. The glory of God is not perfection. It is hard for us to accept this, but this is God's enduring sign for faithful followers whose own bodies have been damaged.

Transfiguration

And he was transfigured before them, and his face shone like the sun, and his clothes became dazzling white.

Matthew 17.2

The divinity of Christ is revealed in the transfiguration on the mountain top. The dazzling light shining from within Jesus is linked to many moments in the history of God when light reveals God or God's glory, such as the creation story, the burning bush, Elijah's chariot of fire (2 Kings 2.9–12), Moses' bright face, the light which blinds Paul at his conversion on the road to Damascus.

Christ is a new creation – not a better version of what has gone before. In the story of Jesus' transfiguration Moses and Elijah are seen by the disciples when they are on the mountain with Jesus. On this mountain Jesus is not passed stone tablets from Moses, instead, Jesus *communes* with the patriarchs. They talk, perhaps in friendship. Jesus explains nothing to those disciples who will be commissioned to go out to speak and serve in his name and in the name of hope. As Jesus dazzles with holiness, the One who sent him speaks on his behalf. The mysterious and previously hidden household of God is revealed in the transfiguration of Jesus. God's Holy Spirit – like a celestial fire – ignites Jesus in radiant splendour.

'This is my Son, the Beloved; with him I am well pleased; listen to him!'

Matthew 17.5

The disciples accompanying Jesus at the transfiguration are unable interpret the events in front of them, yet they are keen to understand what is going on. They try to grasp hold of the patriarchs, suggesting that booths be erected to contain them. They are unable to only behold the glory *as it is*, instead they want to contain and own it.

The response of those disciples who witness the transfiguration surely would have been more fitting if they had only watched and then responded in communion: 'Alleluia Amen.' *Thanks be to God: Yes! Yes!* Jesus wanted them to deeply see God's glory revealed through him. It is moving that, in Matthew's version of this event, Jesus touches them. Like a parent he reassures them. But it is also significant that after communing with the patriarchs and shining with divinity, Jesus passes on to those who would do his will, his divinity with his own hands. Glory is not confined to God any more – it is shared and there is lots to go round. Through baptism, ordination and holding the hands of those who are afraid, confused or dying, we are all successors of that moment when Jesus' body was transfigured by light into glory and physically felt by the disciples whom we try to emulate.

A sick person may not feel that their body is able to be illuminated. Even a hint of glorious light flickering in their own flesh may seem an absurd proposal. Sickness disfigures rather than transfigures, surely? But here we are entering into a different process of understanding our new identities that are imposed on us by illness. Identities are not fixed. The new creation that is ushered in by Christ invites us to discern how to live out our own gift of life that has been uniquely offered and formed by God. We do not need to be determined by society's strictures and mostly patriarchal rules. Chronological time – dictated in a linear, end-facing and predictable pattern – is not God's mode. Instead, a dynamic time is preferred. It is that mode of time known in Greek as *kairos*. *Kairos* time is useful here because it helps us to remember to be awake to what is happening 'right now', such as an experience or event that comes in an unexpected, but *just right* moment. What may initially feel like freakishness among a crowd may later illuminate our uniqueness and fire a new vocation.

We will always be incomplete but sometimes incompleteness can be exciting rather than unnerving. Like the disciples, it is tempting to box ourselves in the dark into some imagined past or stale dim present. If we hope that our bodies represent more than flesh, blood and bones then our sense of incompletion can become a source of joy and creativity. We are always in a state of flux that is not pointing to one neat finishing point when we may be fixed and perfect. We are not determined by death either, although many of us live in perpetual torment of death's sting. With hope that our bodies can be charged with light and our nature renewed, we can, with time, medicine, prayer and endless patience, be re-embodied and illuminate God's glory.

> Father in heaven,
> whose Son Jesus Christ was wonderfully transfigured
> before chosen witnesses upon the holy mountain,
> and spoke of the exodus he would accomplish at Jerusalem:
> give us strength so to hear his voice and bear our cross
> that in the world to come we may see him as he is;
> who is alive and reigns with you,
> in the unity of the Holy Spirit,
> one God, now and for ever. Amen.
> Collect for the Feast of the Transfiguration

Epiphany

The Magus in Eliot's 'The Journey of the Magi', recounting his visit to see the Christ child, is diplomatic when describing the moment when they arrive at the stable in Bethlehem:

> Finding the place; it was (you may say) satisfactory.
> T. S. Eliot

What the magi were hoping to find was not at all what the shining star revealed. The Magus says that the circumstances were 'unpropitious'. They travel at 'the very dead of winter'. The darkness and the chaos surrounding the abstruse birth seems set to diminish the glimmering hope which drew them away from the comforts of home. It wasn't the journey that nearly killed them – though that was a trial. It was the attempt to live a new life *in the light* of the encounter with the child Jesus that hurt the most.

They knew they had to transform the way they lived, the way they thought and crucially, executed power. Their certainties vanished. Alone and far away from the grown man Jesus they had to reimagine their futures while also holding on to the memory of the journey and their vision of the Light of the World. Unsettled, the Magus continues to review what he was led to see. His life is lived in a questioning mode.

> . . . were we led all that way for
> Birth or Death? There was a Birth, certainly,
> We had evidence and no doubt. I had seen birth and death,
> But had thought they were different;

Perhaps our greatest hope should be that we can endure uncertainty, unease and unknowing, no matter how well or uncomfortable our bodies feel. We can't put a percentage on the health and well-being of our post-sickness bodies, however comforting medical statisticians' figures may be to us. Perhaps it is a question of holding our nerve, living in a poised state of being open to how our recovery may progress. This may look like hoping against hope, like groping in the darkness, but faith sometimes is not so different from this.

In the season of Epiphany we mark certain events following Christ's birth which reveal how God makes himself more fully known through the birth of Jesus. These include the visit from the Magi, Jesus' baptism by John, the first miracle of changing water into wine, and Mary and Joseph's visit to the Temple to offer a temple sacrifice in thanksgiving for their son's birth. Forty days after Christmas it is the feast of Candlemas. By then the glow of Christmas has faded and the credit card bill has arrived. It is the final formal piece in our Epiphany puzzle of how and why Jesus is the light of the world. The old man, very close to death, who has prayed in the dark for years holds the Christ child in his hands and knows that the child is *the* longed-for light.

> 'A light for revelation to the gentiles and for glory to your people Israel.'
>
> Luke 2.32

Simeon is not afraid of death or darkness because at last he sees and knows that the long wait is over. At Candlemas church candles are blessed. Their work is crucial in our worship: lit stumps of wax create fragile glory. They are symbols of the divine and a reminder of the treasure of light. Every day millions of candles are lit in churches throughout the world. Even those who reject or know little about the Christian faith seem to be drawn to light a candle. The candles create prayers of their own.

Our experience of illness can mirror the events we review in the Epiphany season. Outsiders are called to visit our own inscrutable bodies in an unfamiliar place such as a hospital; our bodies can be places of sacred potential, as in the wedding at Cana where water is transformed to wine unexpectedly – for generosity alone; we can be the baptized one submitting to chaos and despair and the reality of death; we can be our own Simeon recognizing in the muted light our bodies' capacity for transformation and recovery.

Glimpses of Light

We have to keep our eyes open. Sin is a form of blindness; it is a refusal to see beyond the surface, between the lines, at the edges. Our Christian vocation is to learn to see differently. This requires practice and patience, of course. But most importantly, that which keeps eyes fixed is the *expectation* that something will be found. This is the essence of hope. It is the act of perception and not the moment of reception that drives us, however counter-intuitive and counter-cultural this may seem. We do not look and wait in order to possess; rather, we look and wait to find and be found.

Our eyes must be exposed to light. Unlike the intrepid explorer, we do not have to travel very far in order to see, but we do have to be patient. Perhaps some of us expect too much of our bodies. We want to upgrade them or exchange them for a new model but we are not commodities, but gifts.

Now faith is the assurance of things hoped for, the conviction of things not seen.

Hebrews 11.1

Are we to abandon any hope of improvement once we are reconciled to having wounded, inconvenient and painful bodies? No: hope can be expanded and enlarged. Jesus offered much more than touching and healing disfigured bodies. He reached souls, converted minds, enlightened dull spirits and drew a whole world to God – the light of all lights. Although Christ reveals to us that our bodies really matter, we are encouraged to recognize that we are more than our bodies, our tribe, our brains and bank accounts. We can cling to Christ once we realize that there is not much else – or *anything* – that is so dependable.

It is scientifically proven that my sight will remain impaired. People will always suddenly flash from the left and unknowingly shock and scare me. I will continue to miss a car by a whisker. I open my eyes and do not really see. Perhaps the blindness – the pervasive vacancy caused by bleeding brain cells – could be a presence, revealing how much more there is for me to see. My sight *may* improve if I dare to wait, reflect, remember and hope that I can see God there with me.

Sick people need to be encouraged to keep on hoping that things will get better, even when it becomes quite clear that recovery will be slow or may not ever happen. Are we meant to hope for a miracle? It is a difficult question to answer. If the chemotherapy has failed to eradicate cancer and it has spread to other body parts it may not be our calling to pray for miracles, hoping 'against the odds'. Perhaps we can think of it differently: the word 'miracle' is a synonym for hope, and our prayer could be that the sick person we love can face the physical pain in a comfortable way. Sometimes hope may be the hope for a good death, not a good fight.

This way we can dig for more light in darker places and see that there is light in that most terrifying place: death. Many people fail to grasp this because they believe that death is too final. The true end of our Christian faith is to spend eternity dwelling in God's eternal light. We should probably all hope that our faith will not crack when we really and truly need it the most; that is to say, when we know, *really know*, that death is approaching. If we allow ourselves to be expectant we can begin to prepare for God to journey beside us towards death. Hope allows for a graced death.

Remaking Light

If we are recovering from sickness we need to make sense out of our experiences in relationship with God. We need to see afresh – with eyes transfigured by hope. X-rays, scans, observation, inspection: we can do this endoscopic investigation of ourselves in order to see anew. We can develop heightened sensitivity and dare to imagine more from God and from ourselves. Wakening from despair makes way for a new light to shine from us, in us and on us.

Like prayer, and with prayer, hope can be developed and honed. The development of our faith is a mode of ceaseless searching, discovery and recovery. To be faithful is to attempt to live a receptive life learning and relearning that God is faithful and wonder-full. Prayer begins in hopefulness, otherwise, why would we bother? The One who keeps his promises offers greater riches than the alleviation of pain and physical recovery. We can only see this though if we also look back, look up, look out and away from our mortal bodies. Hope requires a new attunement. Signs of healing must never be restricted to the sealing of our scars or the hospital discharge letter.

We make meaning through the patterning of the past, present and fragile future of our own lives. We try to notice glimmers of God's glory in us and around us. This can be a painstaking task. We need to recall places, moments and search for shapes, *bodily feelings*, moments and events where God has appeared in our lives that we may have ignored, or never dared imagine might be possible. But God breaks in whether we detect it or not. God has been at work giving unearned grace upon grace. In our recovery time, if we attempt to make patterns through remembering and searching in prayer and patience, we may see that new light really does have the potential to change us.

> Your light shone upon me in its brilliance, and I thrilled with love and dread alike.
>
> Augustine, *Confessions*, 7.10

At first the patterns may not look neat or easily fit together. Our sensations, and our half-remembered experiences may appear random or chaotic. What we find may even seem empty, but it *will* fill out as we look back and look out and learn to see our past with new eyes in new light for moments and signs when God was there but we did not see. Hope is created by this work; future expectations grow. Meaning and purpose can be made here as we gather fragments creating an autobiography of the body and soul that may lead us to a body that becomes at peace with itself. Often humility increases as we see how many good gifts we have experienced without seeing God there. At first, hoping begins with humility, not least because we must admit that we can't always see and know. Here perhaps, humility is another word for prayer.

We must salvage our past and our bodies out of the dark and bring them into light. In our recovery we are salvaging ourselves through the painstaking work of waiting and watching, remembering, piecing together and humbly, humbly letting go. We can be in the present, meeting God in the now, because the now is God.

Death and Resurrection

Richard Chartres, the Bishop of London, explained to me that the purpose of theological college is to learn theology and discover how to pray. He was right. I spent three years at Westcott House and the obligation of attendance at Morning Prayer in the chapel has shaped my days and my priesthood ever since. The solid theological foundations set there makes preparing sermons a treat rather than a burden.

Early one evening, only a week before my move from our cramped flat in Brixton to the tranquil garden quad on Jesus Lane, Cambridge, I glanced out of our kitchen window and saw a group of men with their trousers down, injecting heroin into their groins. Entering theological college was like stepping into a fantasy land.

I rarely spoke about my illnesses at Westcott; I was firmly in the closet about my poor health. An obligatory placement in a Cambridge college chapel during my first term resulted in a final report in which the chaplain expressed concern that I had 'issues with personal space'. Indeed I do have problems with the space all around me, but it is not an 'issue': it is my life. I did not bother explaining. Cambridge culture thrives on the survival of the fittest.

The most obvious sign of difference was not my brain, nor my sexuality. It was my accent. My strong northern twang made me a verbal plaything and a Cambridge curiosity for my posh new peers.

I learned just as much about the priesthood in the bar at Westcott House as I did in the university. My fellow ordinands were engaged, articulate and committed; the Divinity Faculty second to none.

My grandfather served as a vicar at a time when lots of people went to church. Yet it seems to me that he spent a lot of time in his vicarage; he never seemed rushed. He and my grandmother took their main meal at lunchtime (which they called dinner), and had a light meal (tea) served on a trolley, with a cosy-covered tea-pot, home-made bread and home-made Victoria sandwich cake. Perhaps he didn't have to try so hard. I know he always prayed. It always shows.

At Westcott House teachers talked endlessly about boundaries and the importance of days off, splitting the day into three blocks – morning, afternoon and evening – and making sure that one of those was spent in rest. Unfortunately, their insistence was not enough for me to take heed. I was certain priesthood was not a job, but a way of life and I am still convinced of that now.

The notion that service to God offered perfect freedom seduced me. I wanted to spend my life in prayer and service to others – and not to myself. I was so thankful, so *grateful* for being alive. The potential of transformation offered daily by the Church's beautiful sacramental liturgy elated me. I pledged to offer my life back to God in an act of sacrifice. I gave my self as a gift in return for the gift of life. I was still living, walking, breathing and thinking. I had a lot to be thankful for.

Like many other clergy I am often asked why I decided to be a priest; my starting point tends to be my brain haemorrhages. The drama of nearly losing my life, finding God and serving God in thanks and praise is a neat enough version for most intrigued enquirers. I am called to defend the Church when I am asked how I feel about its stance on homosexuality and its misogyny. It seems to be getting harder to exonerate the Church as time passes, but I find that personalizing it tends to work.

'The Church,' I say, taking a deep breath to loosen up my palpable defensiveness, 'is a priest burying a widower with only two mourners in the congregation. The Church is a single gay vicar running a parents and toddlers group on a council estate hundreds of miles away from his friends. The Church is a hospital chaplain holding the hand of a dying child. The Church is me talking to you right now.'

After ordination I served as a curate at St Stephen's Rochester Row in Westminster. Soon I began to have nocturnal epileptic seizures. The first time this happened I was meant to be giving an assembly to the poshest prep school in Britain the morning after; needless to say, Amy called and cancelled my appearance on my behalf. She would sometimes go into work late, or not at all, in order to look after me. At that time she was a presenter on the breakfast show on BBC Radio London and when she arrived on air an hour late nobody ever mentioned why. Perhaps people presumed that she had overslept. As a freelancer, Amy lost quite a lot of work and money having to look after me when I had a seizure. My seizures worsened. I began to worry that an epileptic aura may appear when I was preaching in the pulpit. Fighting time and my body, I missed church one Sunday morning and ran the London Marathon a few months before my thirtieth birthday. Never again.

On Fridays, my day off, I often slept till noon, something I never used to do, not least because I always viewed sleeping too much as a waste of precious time: life! It is an act of masochistic hubris – surely – that clergy are expected to have only one day off a week, just like God gave himself a Sabbath rest at the creation. The pressure for clergy to be perfect and flaunt twenty-four-hour sprightliness is pervasive. Clerical collars and non-stop smiley service can cage us rather than set us free. Despite filling me with overpowering joy and relief, it is hard to accept now that being ordained has *made me who I am*, which is often how the vocation to the priesthood is often described. I have cloaked my sexuality and my relationship, I have hidden my physical weaknesses and colluded with the dominant narrative of always putting others before myself. I pushed aside my medical history and neglected my body. However, I now recognize that my weakness is my strength; the source of my compassion for people is my own suffering.

Bishops and ordination selectors are seeking signs of selflessness. They want to test their interviewees' strength of conviction, their willingness *to go the extra mile*. We might interpret this cliché as a metaphor for patient attentiveness to one's prayer life, but that would be naive. They really mean, 'Will you work for a month without a day off if unexpected events occur for which you will be needed?' The notion of running the race that is set before us that is encouraged in the letter to the Hebrews (12.1) is privileged above Jesus' regular disappearances to pray alone or eat and drink with friends.

We have created a white, male, muscular middle-class idol of Christlikeness. The most provocative question we can pose about the (universal) Church's honest belief in the kinds of people God calls to serve as priests is: 'How many centuries will it be before the pope is a black lesbian?' Shocking isn't it?

It has been difficult to admit that my imperfectly glorious body and brain means that I am not fit to be a vicar. I cannot multitask. I have a neuropsychologist's report to prove it, if only to myself. It troubles me that clergy who are not vicars running buoyant parishes are suspected of being inferior examples of priesthood. A day beginning by checking various spreadsheets of financial accounts all morning, followed by lunch with a banker to prise a fat cheque from his pocket to replace the wheezing organ, then rushing back to fix the photocopier to finish the orders of service in time for tomorrow's big memorial service, then chairing a school governors' meeting which finished at 10.30 p.m. would kill me.

As a university chaplain today I spend lots of time with distressed students, mostly absorbing their anxiety. It is a great honour to be trusted in this way. I recognize that offering pastoral support is where my gifts lie. I cannot bump into anyone while sitting in my armchair facing a tense student. I mostly set my own pace; my time and loving attention is my offering to anyone in need. It is in these situations when I feel most free, most gifted and most Christlike. There are no outward signs that I am a wounded healer, and rarely do I tell the students or staff anything about the despair and pain I have suffered. But as I sit with those who weep, who look me in the face asking, *Why?* I do not grope for facile reassurances, but in a very humble way, my body sitting before them as a priest and patient listener is part of the answer.

A Way of Death and Life

But the LORD God called to the man, and said to him, 'Where are you?'

Genesis 3.9

Death surely scares everyone. It is sometimes so frightening to think that we are not able to imagine what it might feel like to die and be dead. If this is so, death is a no-place; it is real but unimaginable and hovers as a dark, looming absence to flee from at any cost. It is understandable because holding on to a vision of life beyond flesh can easily fade.

This *Good News* story of Jesus just may not be true any more. It can be terrifying to live in our bodies if we have abandoned the expectation of an after-death future. If we have lost faith in God's promises and lost trust in our bodies, then imagination, insight and memory need to be harnessed. We can use this in-between time, between recovery and death, to honestly reconcile our faith, our fears and our own bodies with the resurrected body of Christ.

The crucifixion of Christ is a threat to those who strive to curate easy pain-free lives. We want desperately to live, yet we despise our bodies that hold us to ransom, falsely offering us tantalizing snatches of extra time before we perish. It is a pervasive delusion.

If we have lost hope in eternity we may feel easily distanced from our past, which may feel like a time when the threat of death was far off. We may sense that those around us have become dislocated and that the close reality of dying is stretching us away from lively people in our preparation for loneliness. Time may feel at once loved for the opportunities it may provide, and loathed for its limitedness. For those who are healthy existence can easily switch between past, present and future. For the dying person who has forgotten God's history, there is only 'now'.

Our society is death averse. We have spent so much of our lives working to earn money, buy things and do more. Yet we are either too attached to our possessions or too envious of those who will outlive us that it can be easy to overlook making provision for the things we once believed defined us: homes, cars, bank accounts. A third of people over the age of 55 do not have wills. We will go to many lengths to avert our end. Extra time on earth is more accessible to the rich who can opt for expensive last-ditch treatments. In America 40 per cent of oncologists have admitted offering pricey treatments to cancer patients that they knew were unlikely to work. *Not dying yet* is a retail activity.

When death is sensed to be close failure can haunt us, high-lighting moments in our lives where chances were missed, mistakes made and cruelties inflicted. We convict ourselves rather than make peace with ourselves. Fear of death reveals us and we become exposed, naked to the truth. Living out our lives without the hope of forgiveness and transformation is to belong to the old creation.

✠

The trauma of the wilderness created by Adam and Eve's pride persists for those full of fear and guilt. We can identify more than ever with their stupidity and greed and narrow vision. Adam and Eve abused the gifts offered freely to them by God in the garden of Eden. Their pride took away their innocence; they recognized their nakedness and were suddenly ashamed and fearful of their bodies. They felt judged by a God full of wrath rather than generosity. This stage in the creation story can be seen as the moment in the story of our illness when we moved from good health to bad health; from ease to dis-ease. God persists; if we persist we can try to move from the pain, the terror and the fear – towards recovery, change and freedom.

The story has not ended yet.

With faith we wait to meet God in a new place. The moment when God's wish is fulfilled is imagined by John the Divine as the final end of humanity's salvation.

> Then saw a new heaven and a new earth;
> for the first heaven and the first earth had passed away,
> and the sea was no more.
> And I saw the holy city, the new Jerusalem,
> coming down out of heaven from God,
> prepared as a bride adorned for her husband.
> And I heard a loud voice from the throne saying,
> 'See, the home of God is among mortals.
> He will dwell with them;
> they will be his peoples,
> and God himself will be with them;

he will wipe every tear from their eyes.
Death will be no more;
mourning and crying and pain will be no more,
for the first things have passed away.'

Revelation 21.1–4

To be persistent is not to live at all costs, nor to refuse to live life
hampered by thoughts of death. Persistence is best employed in
order to enter more deeply into the dynamic life of God which the
suffering and resurrected Christ reveals.

Then the eyes of both were opened.

Genesis 3.7

Staring Life in the Face

The common phrase of 'staring death in the face' is an interesting
metaphor to describe the experience of coming close to death.
But must it be a metaphor? Christ's dead face is offered for us
to observe and gape at. Every crucifix invites the viewer to see
God being dead. God, who is revealed as *being* itself. We have
seen that 'I AM' becomes an 'it' in the cross, a mere object among
others. Perhaps staring at Christ's dead face offends us. It is the
body of an excruciating failure and a symbol of farce. Jesus' gaunt
stoniness may terrify us all the more. But God invites us *not* to
turn away as God asked Moses to do when he gave the people of
Israel the Ten Commandments which explained clearly, though
not simply, how to live and how to please God. To stare at the
God of Israel meant to die. God said to Moses,

'you cannot see my face; for no one shall see me and live.'

Exodus 33.20

Looking at the dead Messiah we can learn to die well. Christ's
crucified body depicted in sculptures and paintings and millions
of other objects is concave and sharply chiselled, emphasizing his
lifelessness. There is no prettiness now. This is not a sign of life

or hope at all if we fix our eyes on the crucifix out of context or disconnected from past and future. Crucially, his dead face and disfigured body hanging on a cross over a desolate rubbish heap is not an end in itself, just as Adam and Eve's transgression was not. This is part of Christ's Way, where death is *creative*. The dead body of Jesus on barren land is not even a stumbling block: if we follow Christ and walk, it is the path to new life.

Thou dost hold before our eyes a corpse yet the very source of life.

Greek Orthodox liturgy

A New Eden

For as all die in Adam, so all will be made alive in Christ.

1 Corinthians 15.22

Christ's public journey began with a baptism; he was plunged into the dark watery chaos of death. Publicly and symbolically he enters into the world of death and the judgement of others. Returning out of the water is a metaphoric rebirth; here he is named and addressed by God: 'You are my Son, the Beloved; with you I am well pleased' (Mark 1.11). Jesus' torture and death only three years later is by no means a metaphor at all. Jesus' flesh is broken by nails, he stops breathing, goes stiff and is laid in a tomb.

It is dawn when the women go to the tomb to anoint Jesus' dead body. Dawn: that in-between time, that cusp point in the day when the dying tend to slip away. This first light time is the dawning of a very new creation. The rolled-away stone creates a gash, a rupture that initially does not seem at all propitious. Yet it is here where Adam and Eve are released from the imprisonment of shame. Matthew writes that at the resurrection an earthquake occurred (28.2). The earth shifts and is realigned.

At first the tomb is barren in its emptiness. It sits in the lush garden but is filled with a puzzling absence: the dead body of Jesus has gone. Mary Magdalene, the outsider of outsiders – a woman and a prostitute – displays the surest sticking power: she holds her nerve. It is often the case that the least powerful persevere and *see things differently*. Perhaps the trauma of persistent shame enables her to endure her churning gut and heart-in-the-mouth horror, and stay put. Outsiders do not always trust reason so perhaps she knows well that disorder can offer significant possibilities. Mystery and unknowing can be treasured possessions for outsiders. People who are ill may identify with Mary here because those whose sick bodies seem pushed to the margins by the healthy centre sometimes learn to sit through terror and look expectantly for new life in unlikely places. A gash in the flesh makes way for a birth; twined thorns form a crown; dead wood flourishes into a blossoming tree; an opened tomb hatches new life.

The soldiers guarding the tomb in Matthew's account see the risen Christ and become 'like dead men' (Matthew 28.4) because they cannot see beyond the stable and the ordinary. Incomprehensibility and shock pierce their sides: they are frightened to death by fear.

Good health is never a fact, only a possibility. If we recover when medics frowned and swore we could not, is it a miracle, or is it our pluck that saved us from death, for now at least? Mystery matters and imagination counts more than many reckon. The resurrection of Christ is not a fact to be investigated, nor is it a miracle to be proved. We learn to trust the anaesthetist staring down on us to pump drugs so that we will not feel our flesh being knifed open. This may not be so different from an attempt to allow God's resurrection to be part of our lives. It is perhaps a process, and a sensation of letting go. Jesus' resurrection body is not a resuscitated body, though when we are close to death that may be what we hope for ourselves. New life means more than 'made better' again. Therefore, to see Christ's risen body we must look tangentially, using our memories and our hearts to see and know that we are not abandoned. The resurrection does not offer us proof of the afterlife, but it does reassure us that God is faithful to his promises.

Alone, Mary Magdalene walks in the garden where the tomb yawns open. She is alert as she weeps but despondent at the thought that Jesus' body has been stolen. Her perseverance contrasts with the behaviour of the disciples who, only a few days before, slept in the garden of Gethsemane while Jesus cried in terrified expectation of his death. It was in that garden where Jesus admitted to his terror of impending death: 'I am deeply grieved, even to death' (Matthew 26.38). That moment in the Garden of Gethsemane is startling, even scandalous. His terror of death throws him to the ground of his Father's own making. Jesus' body lying on the ground and his tears watering it signals the birth pangs of God's new creation: Jesus' humble body and the humus of decomposing earth conjoin.

> Faithfulness will spring up from the ground,
>   and righteousness will look down from the sky.
>
> Psalm 85.11

The Resurrection Garden

The man Mary sees in the garden must look at peace with the garden because she presumes that the risen Christ is the gardener. Her body becomes dynamic because John tells us that she turns twice, as though she is preparing for important events to bombard her. As the first witness of the resurrection her physical movements combine with the seismic transformation that is revealed before her eyes. The world which will come to learn of and believe in God's resurrection and love turns with her body; her body becomes the earth's axis for a moment. Yet as she turns towards Jesus the exchange is not cosmic, but intimate. Jesus speaks first and names her. The stone blocking her vision is rolled away from her eyes. Mary immediately gives him a title in return: 'dearest teacher'. Now she knows it is he, the one she followed and loved. Her mind and her hands would still contain the memory of caressing and tending to his feet in the upper room. It is understandable that her instinct is to touch him once again and tend to his fresh wounds. But this wasn't a body in the way that it was before the crucifixion.

> 'Have you seen him whom my soul loves?'
> Scarcely had I passed them,
> When I found him whom my soul loves.
> I held him, and would not let him go.
>
> Song of Solomon 3.3–4

'I have seen the Lord!' Mary proclaims; she experiences a baptism and resurrection in that moment when she is named and he is recognized. Combining insight with experience she believes, despite her confusion. Next, she obeys him and does his will.

It may be frustrating for us, but the risen Christ does not explain who he is, he *reveals* who he is. The resurrection of Christ is oblique, but then good religion is like that. The word 'religion' comes from the Latin, *religare*, which means to 'bind'; so we have to make connections both ourselves and together in communities. This resurrection Way is a way of life rooted in faithfulness, upon ground created by God, tilled by Christ the Son and enriched by the Spirit.

> Do not fear, for I have redeemed you;
>   I have called you by name, you are mine.
>
> Isaiah 43.1

Those who had followed Jesus are confused and distressed. They run away, but it is Christ who perseveres, and just as God approached Adam, so Christ finds, greets and forgives those who misunderstood and abandoned him. He is 'I AM' revealed among them again, but he is One who is renewed and transfigured. When Jesus meets the disciples he helps them make further connections: 'it is I myself,' he says, emphasizing that it is really him (Luke 24.39). Yet the risen Christ is not a projection because at first they do not recognize him. There is a discontinuity to him yet a continuity too because his wounds are signs of recognition and the wounds have not disappeared.

The resurrection of Christ offers us further paradoxes to confront, welcome and eventually celebrate. Edward Shillito was a soldier in World War One; the scars of Jesus speak to the wounded men. The resurrection of Jesus whose transformed body retains its wounds is the ultimate and complete sign that our bodies bear God and that there is more to us than suffering flesh and flowing blood.

> The other gods are strong; but thou wast weak;
> They rode but thou didst stumble to a throne;

But to our wounds only God's wounds can speak,
And not a god has wounds, but thou alone.

Edward Shillito, 'Jesus of the Scars'

The risen Jesus causes those whom he meets to review their past and to reinterpret the Old Testament. This is a reminder to us that we must see beyond what is first presented to us. On the road to Emmaus days after the crucifixion of Jesus the disciples recognize Jesus when, after walking alongside them, he breaks bread. Memories resurface of the miracle of the feeding of the 5,000 and the Last Supper, where Jesus broke bread with them and said it represented his body. Once they have recognized him they no longer see that the death of Jesus is discontinuous with the man beside them, nor is his return disconnected from everything that has gone before. As Jesus sits with these confused disciples whom he found walking dejectedly away from Jerusalem, he shows them how to reinterpret the Torah, the prophets and the psalms. They are provided with tools to recognize that every part of it points towards the One – the resurrected Jesus – who is with them. Luke is emphatic when he describes the experience of these disciples who *see* who Jesus now is:

Then their eyes were opened, and they recognized him.

Luke 24.31

Rising in Peace

Adam and Eve's ignorance and foolishness led God to meet and question them. This encounter opened their eyes to their rebellion. The disciples' opened eyes lead to reconciliation and celebration. Having open eyes is much more than observation. The disciples who meet Jesus on the road also explain to Jesus that their hearts are burning – their response is physical too. We can see truth with other body parts too: our gut, ears, hands, heart and breath. We learn and know with much more than our minds. We can't inspect Christ's resurrection. We can't domesticate Jesus' transfigured body and God's irrepressible glory, but trusting in it can equip us to see in hopeful expectation, rather than observe scientifically and prove that we are right.

'Touch me and see; for a ghost does not have flesh and bones as you see that I have.'

Luke 24.39

For those who have battled with death or those who feel inundated by pain it can be difficult to admit that both death and life are at work in the body in a constant flow. The risen Christ's body is offered as a touchstone of such realities where recovery means much more than survival alone. The more we ingest and look at Jesus' transformed body, the more we begin to make peace with death that will certainly, certainly happen.

Our days can be seen as microcosms of our lives. We see the close of each day of our lives as a death and commendation to God in the hope and expectation of a new day – a resurrection and eternity shared with God. We can mourn our dying bodies in life and so, with thanksgiving, commend ourselves to God, just as we do a dead body at a funeral. The Church's liturgies teach us to see our days in this way, though for many of us today it may appear macabre. It is good to prepare to Rest In Peace when the sun has set.

At the Compline service we find that we have the last words of Jesus on the cross as our last words spoken that day:

Into your hands, O Lord, I commend my spirit.

Yet the opening words of Morning Prayer begin with a proclamation of praise and thanksgiving:

O Lord open our lips, and our mouths shall proclaim your praise.

We are awake, alive; we have risen, and our ultimate life's task is to rejoice with God who is the beginning and end of all life. Each new day is an invitation to be charged with resurrection light.

The night is far gone, the day is near. Let us then lay aside the works of darkness and put on the armour of light.

Romans 13.12

Resurrection bodies are living breathing people – human beings who feel fully alive just as they are right there in the present moment. Illness can shock us into thinking for the first time about our death and the possibility of an afterlife. We can be compelled to review our lives and change them – sometimes radically. We can recognize that our bodies have been dormant like seeds, created by God, but nevertheless nesting, under-nurtured in what was previously felt to be a considerably comfortable condition. The body's beauty, potential and uniqueness can be hidden beneath the surface. Perhaps its surroundings are not suited to its flourishing, so it rests, unknowingly, blindly beneath the light. *Almost* dying can often make us become fully alive. The ground beneath our feet shifts: what we thought we needed to get by each day, and what we learn is essential to survival, changes our landscape. Our wounds are still raw, our pain has not necessarily lessened, but the whole of us is beginning to transform and grow within. We grow because we died; illness enlivens us. Christ's resurrection is our forerunner. We are a new creation and our bodies are new gardens, new Ways to walk with Christ. Faithfulness is about going deeper into our own bodies: digging deep. To honour our surviving bodies is to honour and reveal the risen Christ who wells within us like a dayspring.

The night is far gone, the day is near. Let us then lay aside the works of darkness and put on the armour of light; let us live honourably as in the day.

Romans 13.12–13

The resurrection leaves us with loose ends though. The resurrection does not protect us completely. While Paul's ingenious metaphor of the 'armour of light' (Romans 13.12) might appear combative and defensive, the armour is an image to help us enlighten our bodies from within us. It is easy to become obsessed with ravishing death and darkness, especially when we feel vulnerable. The divine spark within us is there for us to treasure and set free. Trying to live life in the light of the resurrection is a work of art. The transformed crucified body of Jesus invites us to embrace a creative notion of the end of our lives.

> Do you not know that you are God's temple and that God's Spirit dwells in you?
>
> 1 Corinthians 3.16

New Vines in the New Creation

> A shoot shall come out from the stock of Jesse,
>   and a branch shall grow out of his roots.
>
> Isaiah 11.1

Jesus tells Mary Magdalene, 'Go!' The risen Jesus commissions his disciples. He calls them brothers; they are adopted into the family tree whose roots rest in the Father's creation, beginning with Abraham, the great patriarch. Jesus breathes on those who haven't abandoned hope in him, enriching this new creation, just as the Father's breath birthed the world (Genesis 1.2). The disciples' transformation transmits God's forgiveness and peace through their bodies. Their calling is to be physical, to flourish and bear fruit both individually and together.

The new creation is more than just a nice idea. These fruits of the resurrected Christ were shared and passed on throughout the world. In our baptism the priest's hands touch us, commissioning us to share God's tenderness with others. Christ's wounded hands which took, blessed and broke bread with his terrified disciples have been *handed down* to us. Those who saw the risen wounded Christ were sent to tell others what he looked like and what it felt like to be there. They were sent out into danger with only their bodies as a home. As the borders of the new creation were expanding through them and the armour of light they wore unleashed transformation for the world, it did not provide them with protection. Their bodies would be wounded and slaughtered for their commitment to Christ's resurrection.

We may feel far removed from the drama of the post-resurrection events but we are not a passive audience. The resurrection events that we read and try to internalize is not a good yarn for us to call to mind when we are nagged and kept awake by the gnawing fear of death. The risen man they were enthralled by is what love looks like. The dynamic life of God in Trinity is not confined to 'then'. The resurrection is here and now.

'This is why I have let you live: to show you my power and to make my name resound through all the earth.'

Exodus 9.16

Exploring the New Garden

There is a garden at the heart of the new creation birthed by the life, death and resurrection of Christ. It is not a wilderness place where this journey began soon after we became ill and our bodies hurt, and it is by no means a desert. But neither is it a neat finished garden, primped and pretty, walled and private. It is not very dangerous, but neither is it safe or predictable. It is possible to become lost but there is no tricky maze, only peaceful paths that do not lead anywhere in particular. Breezes flow through it and some plants seem to make music. The light shines frequently, though there is also rain and shadow. The garden is diverse and in places it is wild. In other areas it is tamed, pruned and trimmed in order for the old to die and for new growth to be set free. There is a rose garden and a pond with a small fountain. In some places little grows easily. It is not always glorious but it is often beautiful and even beguiling. Its colours burst with *yes*. Other plants take more time to appreciate. The garden bears rich fruit in rich soil and provides shelter and rest for others.

In the middle of this garden there is a tree whose roots run deep beneath the surface. There are scars on the trunk and the tree's life is gradually revealed as the seasons change. Strangely, it buds in the winter but blossoms in spring.

A gardener is always present. He is persistent and attentive; patient and alert. He waits for growth and knows the needs of each plant well. He makes his home at the foot of the tree. He walks, silent and smiling along the paths, but can often be seen under canopies sitting with lightly closed eyes.

Resting in a Windswept Garden

I worry about dying. I do not know what will happen to me when I die but this uncertainty does not seem at odds with my attempts to live out my belief in God, who is most fully revealed in the person of Jesus. It may be most true for me to say that I am hopeful but not so expectant. I hope that I will glorify God in my transfigured and wounded body, lit up by one endless divine light. Perhaps I will feel more ready to die as the years pass and my body loses even more strength. I learned to fight death when I was young, and death shrieks by each time a seizure rushes angrily inside me. Death feels familiar but it is by no means a friend yet.

Some people say that they are not afraid of dying but they are afraid of being in pain. I have a very high pain threshold but I am hopeful that my death will not be sudden. I want to say goodbye. I also want to be able to confess my sins and regrets to someone who will hold me with hands that have anointed the newborn, the dying, the baptized, with wrists that have been lifted up to break bread and shared it with friends and strangers. I hope that I will have the gift of time to renew the promises my parents made for me at my baptism on my behalf: I turn to Christ, I repent of my sins, I renounce evil.

I am almost certain about where I will be buried. There is a cemetery on the edge of Haslingden Moor in Lancashire. There is a Catholic side where my Father's family are buried, and a Protestant side where my maternal grandparents lie in ashes. It is a raw patch of land, half the size of a football pitch. Most often it is freighted with boulder-sized clouds the colour of granite that frequently crack open releasing sheets of rain. Its glory is seen in its honesty: there is no hiding, little shelter and beauty is certainly in the eye of the beholder. The sky is tremendous; the wind blasts. It is too exposed for pretty emblems; there is no rose garden. For some who may visit to place flowers on a family grave, as I do with my parents from time to time, this bleak spot where bodies disappear into the waterlogged ground, might confirm that their end is simply beneath their cold feet. For others like me, the cemetery's uncompromised exposure to the earth's vital elements offers an honest and honourable end point for a new beginning.

> The LORD will guide you continually,
>> and satisfy your needs in parched places,
>> and make your bones strong;
> and you shall be like a watered garden,
>> like a spring of water,
>> whose waters never fail.

Isaiah 58.11

References and Acknowledgements

The publisher and author are grateful for permission to use extracts from published sources under copyright, and have made every effort to trace sources. Do please contact the publisher if any are not included.

T. S. Eliot, 'The Love Song of Alfred J. Prufrock', 'The Waste Land' and 'Journey of the Magi', 2002, *Collected Poems 1909–62*, London: Faber & Faber. Used by permission.

Heaney, Seamus, 2001, 'Miracle', in *Human Chain*, London: Faber & Faber. Used by permission.

Meehan, Paula, 1991, 'Child Burial', in *The Man Who Was Marked By Winter*, Oldcastle, Co. Meath: Gallery Press. Used by permission of Dedalus Press, www.dedaluspress.com.

Shillito, Edward, 1919, 'Jesus of the Scars', in *Jesus of the Scars, and Other Poems*, London: Hodder & Stoughton.

Thomas, R. S., 2000 (new edn), 'Country Clergy', 'The Bright Field' and 'The Absence', in *Collected Poems: 1945–1990*, London: Weidenfeld & Nicolson. Used by permission.

Wannenwetsch, Bernd (ed.), 2009, Bonhoeffer, Dietrich, 2009, *Who am I? Bonhoeffer's Theology through his Poetry*, London: Bloomsbury.

Ward, Benedicta (trans.), 1975, *The Sayings of the Dessert Fathers*, Collegeville, MN: St John's Abbey Liturgical Press.

Watt, Jean M., 'Lent', in Jenny Robertson, (ed.), 1989, *A Touch of Flame: An Anthology of Contemporary Christian Poetry*, Oxford: Lion. Copyright administrator untraced at time of press.

Williams, Rowan, 2002, 'Advent Calendar', in *The Poems of Rowan Williams*, Manchester: Carcanet Press. Used by permission of the Right Reverend Rowan Williams.

Further Reading

Anon., *The Cloud of Unknowing*, available in many editions.

Augustine, 1961, *The Confessions*, trans. Pine-Coffin, R. S., London: Penguin.

Althaus Reid, Marcella, 2004, *From Feminist Theology to Indecent Theology*, London: SCM Press.

Boltz-Weber, Nadia, 2015, *Accidental Saints: Finding God in All the Wrong People*, New York: Convergent Press.

Bonhoeffer, Dietrich, 1978, *Christ the Centre*, trans. Robertson, Edwin H., San Francisco: Harper Collins.

Bonhoeffer, Dietrich, 2002, *Letters and Papers from Prison: An Abridged Version*, London: SCM Press.

Brook, Brian and Swinton, John, 2012, *Disability in the Christian Tradition: A Reader*, Grand Rapids, MI: Eerdmans Publishing Company.

Burrell, B. D. and Ropper, Allan, 2014, *Reaching Down the Rabbit Hole: Extraordinary Journeys into the Human Brain*, London: Atlantic Books.

Burrows, Ruth, 2010, *The Essence of Prayer*, London: Continuum.

Clare, John, 2007, *Poems Selected by Paul Farley*, London: Faber & Faber.

Davies, Oliver and Turner, Denys (eds), 2002, *Silence and the Word: Negative Theology and Incarnation*, Cambridge: Cambridge University Press.

Diski, Jenni, 2017, *In Gratitude*, London: Bloomsbury.

Eliot, T. S., 2001, *Four Quartets*, London: Faber & Faber.

Eliot, T. S., 2002, *Collected Poems 1909–1962*, London: Faber & Faber.

Gooder, Paula, 2016, *Body: Biblical Spirituality for the Whole Body*, London: SPCK.

Grant, Colin, 2016, *A Smell of Burning: The Story of Epilepsy*, London: Jonathan Cape.

Gwande, Atul, 2014, *Being Mortal: Illness, Medicine and What Matters in the End*, London: Profile Books, in association with Wellcome Collection.

Hauerwas, Stanley, 2005, *Cross-Shattered Christ: Meditations on the Seven Last Words*, London: Darton, Longman & Todd.

Heaney, Seamus, 2010, *The Human Chain*, London: Faber & Faber.

Hull, John M., 2013, *Touching the Rock*, London: SPCK.

James, Clive, 2016, *Poetry Notebook: 2006–2014*, London: Pan Macmillan, Picador.

John of the Cross, 2001, *The Poems of St John of the Cross*, trans. Jones, Kathleen, London: Burns & Oates.

Julian of Norwich, 1998, *Revelations of Divine Love*, trans. Spearing, Elizabeth, London: Penguin.

McGilchrist, Iain, 2010, *The Master and his Emissary*, New Haven, CT and London: Yale University Press.

Marsh, Henry, 2014, *Do No Harm: Stories of Life, Death and Brain Surgery,* London: Weidenfeld & Nicholson.

Mayne, Michael, 2006, *The Enduring Melody*, London: Darton, Longman & Todd.

Nouwen, Henri, 1996, *Can you Drink the Cup?*, Notre Dame, IN: Ave Maria Press.

Nouwen, Henri J. M., 2002, *The Wounded Healer*, London: Darton, Longman & Todd.

Sacks, Oliver, 2009, *Seeing Voices: A Journey into the World of the Deaf*, London: Pan Macmillan.

Tolstoy, Leo, 1987, *A Confession and Other Religious Writing*, London: Penguin.

Turner, Denys, 2011, *Julian, Theologian*, New Haven, CT and London: Yale University Press.

Vanier, Jean, 1988, *Broken Body: Journey to Wholeness*, London: Darton, Longman & Todd.

Vanstone, W. H., 2004, *The Stature of Waiting*, London: Darton, Longman & Todd.

Williams, Rowan, 2003, *Silence and Honey Cakes: The Wisdom of the Desert*, Oxford: Lion.

Williams, Rowan, 2014, *The Wound of Knowledge*, London: Darton Longman & Todd.

Williams, Rowan, 2016, *On Augustine*, London: Bloomsbury.

Young, Frances, 2014, *Arthur's Call: A Journey of Faith in the Face of Severe Learning Disability*, London: SPCK.